ACCLAIM

THE SHORTEST HISTO... ...

A *Der Spiegel* "Most Provoking Book of the Year" (2018)

"A must-read."—*The Economist*

"A marvelously concise effort, especially compelling as Angela Merkel is set to step down in 2021, leaving an uncertain vacuum in Europe."—*Kirkus Reviews*

"Hawes does a good job guiding readers . . . pointing out parallels to today and arguing that Germany's history, long-ago and recent, makes it a key, if not *the key*, player in world leadership."—*Booklist*

"Breezy yet knowledgeable, the book provides a thorough grounding in the major historical events and religious and regional differences that shaped the country at the very heart of Europe."—*Foreword*

"A rapid-paced, thought-provoking, easy-to-digest account of German history."—*Library Journal*

"Sweeping and confident . . . has a frightening urgency."
—*Observer*

"Engaging . . . I suspect I shall remember it for a lifetime."
—*The Oldie*

"Fascinating . . . as an introduction to the most important country in Europe today, this is a great read, and an ideal primer."—*Tribune* magazine

"An excellent little book . . . [Hawes] knows what he's on about and his conclusions are measured, but he favors clear, concise prose over dense academese. He has a sense of humor, and a sharp eye for similarities between then and now."—*Spectator*

"Yes, the Nazis are here, but so too is a history stretching from the Germanic tribes who took on the Roman Empire, right up to Chancellor Angela Merkel. . . . Comprehensive, vivid, and entertaining . . . if you want to understand a country on which much of the free world is now pinning its hopes, you could do worse than start here."—*Irish Examiner*

"Here is Germany as you've never known it: a bold thesis; an authoritative sweep and an exhilarating read. Agree or disagree, this is a must for anyone interested in how Germany has come to be the way it is today."
—**Karen Leeder**, professor of modern German literature, University of Oxford

"A daring attempt to remedy the ignorance of the centuries in little over 200 pages . . . not just an entertaining canter past the most prominent landmarks in German history— also a serious, well-researched and radical rethinking of the continuities in German political life."
—**Nicholas Boyle**, Schröder Professor of German, University of Cambridge, *The Tablet*

"Brexit and Trump have given this sweeping story of Germany's struggles with its demons an urgent topicality. For as Hawes knows better than anyone, if there is a future for liberal democracy, it will be a German one."
—**Nick Cohen**, *Observer* columnist

THE
SHORTEST
HISTORY
OF
GERMANY

THE
SHORTEST
HISTORY
OF
GERMANY

**From Julius Caesar to Angela Merkel—
A Retelling for Our Times**

JAMES HAWES

THE EXPERIMENT

NEW YORK

The Experiment, LLC
220 East 23rd Street, Suite 600, New York, NY 10010-4658
theexperimentpublishing.com

THE EXPERIMENT and its colophon are registered trademarks of The Experiment, LLC. Many of the designations used by manufacturers and sellers to distinguish their products are claimed as trademarks. Where those designations appear in this book and The Experiment was aware of a trademark claim, the designations have been capitalized.

The Experiment's books are available at special discounts when purchased in bulk for premiums and sales promotions as well as for fund-raising or educational use. For details, contact us at info@theexperimentpublishing.com.

Library of Congress Cataloging-in-Publication Data

Names: Hawes, J. M. (James M.) author.
Title: The shortest history of Germany : from Julius Caesar to Angela Merkel : a retelling for our times / James Hawes.
Description: New York : Experiment, [2019] | Originally published: United Kingdom : Old Street Publishing, 2017. | Includes index.
Identifiers: LCCN 2018054456 (print) | LCCN 2018055854 (ebook) | ISBN 9781615195701 (ebook) | ISBN 9781615195695 (pbk.)
Subjects: LCSH: Germany--History.
Classification: LCC DD17 (ebook) | LCC DD17 .H39 2019 (print) | DDC 943--dc23
LC record available at https://lccn.loc.gov/2018054456

ISBN 978-1-61519-569-5
Ebook ISBN 978-1-61519-570-1

Cover design by Sarah Smith | Text design by Old Street Publishing, LTD
Cover illustration, and original maps and illustrations by James Nunn

Manufactured in the United States of America

First printing March 2019
10 9 8 7 6 5 4 3

To the memory of my father, Maurice Hawes,
and the future of my third son,
Karl Maurice Hawes v. Oppen,
whose lives crossed for a few hours on February 25, 2015

CONTENTS

If Not Now, When?

The West is in full retreat. The Anglo-Saxon powers, great and small, withdraw into fantasies of lost greatness. Populists all over Europe cry out that immigration and globalization are the work of a nefarious System, run by unseen masters with no national loyalties. Hardly believing his luck, Tsar Vladimir watches his Great Game line up; the Baltic and Vizegrad states shiver. Germany's Foreign Minister from 1998–2005 sees very little hope left:

> Europe is far too weak and divided to stand in for the US strategically; and, without US leadership the West cannot survive. Thus, the Western world as virtually everyone alive today has known it will almost certainly perish before our eyes.
>
> Joschka Fischer, *The End of the West*, Dec. 5, 2016

Meanwhile, a *New York Times* headline wonders whether the *Liberal West's Last Defender* might be Angela Merkel, Chancellor of Germany.

Germany? The land where, within living memory, Adolf Hitler was quasi-democratically confirmed in power (though only just, and only thanks to a very specific group of voters, as we'll see) and proceeded to unleash all-out war in pursuit of a murderously racist dominion? Can Germany really have changed so drastically in a single lifetime?

Yes, it can. But to understand this—and why Germany may now be our last hope—we have to throw away a great deal of what we think we know about German history, and start afresh.

So let's begin at the very beginning. Or rather, a little further back, at the *proto*-beginning . . .

In the Proto-Beginning

Around 500 BC, at our best guess, in a collection of Iron Age huts in southern Scandinavia or northernmost Germany, one branch of the Indo-European population of Europe began to pronounce certain consonants differently from everyone else.

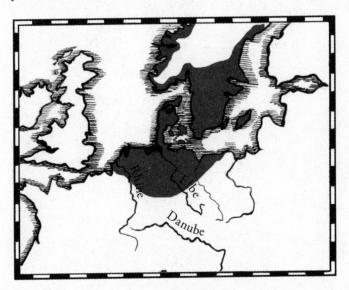

Where it probably started, c. 500 BC.

Exactly who and where and when and why, nobody knows for sure, or ever can. We can, though, reconstruct *what* happened. Take those question-words. Other languages went on using a *c/k/qu* sound (as in the Latin *quis, quid, quo, cur, quam*) and still do today (*quoi, que, che, kakiya* and so on); but the ancestor of Danish, English, German and suchlike now peeled off and started using a *hv/wh/h* sound, leading to the modern *hvad/what/was* and so on.

The *First Germanic Sound-Shift* is also known as *Grimm's Law* because it was set down by Jacob, elder of the folktale-collecting Brothers Grimm. Its effect can most clearly be seen in modern English, which uses both Germanic and non-Germanic, Latin-derived versions.

p became f:	paternal – fatherly
f became b:	fraternal – brotherly
b became p:	labia – lip
c/k/qu became hv/wh/h:	century – hundred
h became g:	horticulture – gardening
g became k:	gnostic – know
t became th:	triple – three
d became t:	dental – teeth

The tribes who (we deduce) started using these new sounds in about 500 BC are known as the *proto-Germans*. We have no idea what they called themselves, because at this stage they had no contact whatever with the peoples of the Mediterranean, who had things like aqueducts, libraries, theaters, elections and written history.

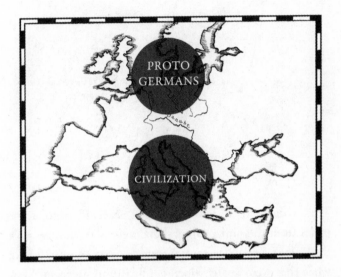

We do know that by about 150 BC, the proto-Germans had started interacting with the Mediterranean world. From this period, Roman-made wine-drinking sets start turning up all over Germany. We also know that shopping was a new experience for them, because in all Germanic languages, the word for buying things (*kaupa/kopen/shopping/kaufen* etc.) is taken straight from the Latin word *caupo,* which means *small trader or innkeeper.* We can imagine First Contact taking place in some trading post on the Rhine or the Danube, where the proto-German elite exchanged furs, amber, their blond hair (prized by Roman wig-makers) and above all slaves, for drink.

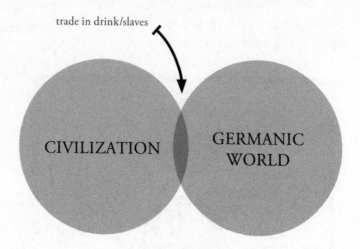

trade in drink/slaves

CIVILIZATION

GERMANIC WORLD

This trade seems to have continued peacefully until some tribes from the north called the *Cimbri* and *Teutones* gave the Roman Republic a mortal scare from 112 BC until 101 BC, when they were finally wiped out by the great general Marius. Later patriots would claim them as early Germans, but to the Romans they were just generic barbarians. Certainly, no one ever called them *Germans* at the time. In fact, as far as we know, no one ever called anyone a German until 58 BC. Fittingly, the whole grand story starts with one of the most famous men in history.

PART ONE

The First Half-Millennium: 58 BC–526 AD

*The Romans Create the Germans,
Then the Germans Take Over Rome*

Caesar Invents the Germans

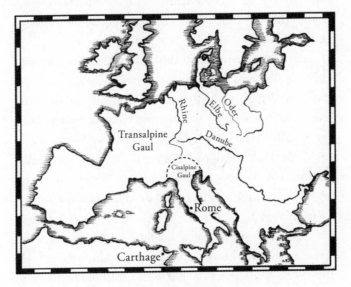

Rome and Gaul before Caesar.

In March 60 BC, the main topic of conversation in Rome (wrote the philosopher-lawyer-politician Cicero) was the threat of barbarian asylum seekers. They were flooding into the already Romanized area of Cisalpine Gaul—in essence, today's northern Italy—because of unrest and wars further north. There seemed to be a new and troublesome power in unconquered Transalpine Gaul. In 58 BC, Julius Caesar, the new governor of Cisalpine Gaul, itching for a war of conquest to make his reputation and clear his debts, gave them a name: *Germani*.

From the first mention on page one of his bestselling history, the *Gallic War,* Caesar firmly pairs these *Germani* with the idea that they *dwell beyond the Rhine.* He is filling in a map as blank for his own readership as Central Africa was for Sir Henry Morton Stanley's, and he gets his big idea in straight away. Rome and Gaul overlap, both physically and culturally, but beyond the Rhine lies a completely different nation. This is hammered home throughout the pages of the *Gallic War.*

Caesar soon discovers that things are indeed looking bad. Some Gaulish tribes had bribed 15,000 fighting Germans across the Rhine to help them against the domineering Aedui. But having won the day, the German leader, Ariovistus, called more of his people across the Rhine and is now *de facto* ruler of all non-Roman Gaul. There are already 120,000 Germans in Gaul; soon, more will come and drive out the locals, who will be forced to seek new homes.

Patriot that he is, Caesar immediately sees the danger. The Roman province of Cisalpine Gaul—maybe even Rome itself—will be swamped by barbarian migrants. He inspires his quailing legionaries with a splendid oration and advances, carefully avoiding the dreaded narrow roads and forests. The tribes he collectively terms the *Germani* are engaged at the *Battle of Vosges* in 58 BC.

The Germans are utterly beaten and, as usual in premodern warfare, rout turns into general slaughter. When the survivors flee across the river, Caesar wants to go after them. The Ubii (Germans, but allies of Rome) offer to ferry his army over the Rhine. Caesar decides it would be more Roman, and safer, to build a bridge across the river. His legions do so in ten days, a quite astonishing feat.

However awe-inspiring Rome's military tech, though, it comes down to boots on the ground. And the Germans know this ground. They escape into the forests, where, Caesar learns, they plan to gather all their forces and await the Roman attack. At this, having advanced far enough to serve (as he neatly spins it) both honor and polity, Caesar returns into Gaul, cutting down the bridge behind him.

For the rest of the *Gallic War*, the Germans lurk as potential allies of anyone in Gaul who wants to rebel. There's only one solution: let them feel the full might of Rome. So when, in 55 BC, they attempt a mass migration across the Rhine, Caesar resolves to *make war against the Germans*.

Caesar boasts that his troops came back *safe to a man* after driving 430,000 of the enemy into the deadly confluence of the Rhine and the Meuse, *where they perished*. Even by Roman standards, this was clearly a massacre, not a war. The great orator, Cato, publicly demanded that Caesar be handed over to the Germans as punishment. But Caesar uses the *Gallic War* to justify the brutality of his methods as an effective deterrent: when the rebellious Gauls next try to bribe the Germans over, the Germans reply that they are not going to risk it after what happened last time.

What, then, are these newly discovered barbarians really like? Caesar pauses his action-packed tale at suitably dramatic moment—he's standing at his second bridgehead across the Rhine, in 53 BC—to give his readers his famous description, the first in history, of the Germans.

Caesar's Germans

The Germans differ much [from the Gauls] for they have neither Druids to preside over sacred offices, nor do they pay great regard to sacrifices. They rank in the number of the gods those alone whom they behold, and by whose instrumentality they are obviously benefitted, namely, the sun, fire, and the moon; they have not heard of the other deities even by report. Their whole life is occupied in hunting and in the pursuits of the military art . . . they bathe promiscuously in the rivers and [only] use skins or small cloaks of deer's hides, a large portion of the body being in consequence naked. They do not pay much attention to agriculture, and a large portion of their food consists in milk, cheese, and flesh; nor has anyone a fixed quantity of land or his own individual limits . . . They consider this the real evidence of their prowess, that their neighbors shall be driven out of their lands and abandon them, and that no one dare settle near them . . . Robberies which are committed beyond the boundaries of each state bear no infamy . . . To injure guests they regard as impious; they defend from wrong those who have come to them for any purpose whatever, and esteem them inviolable; to them the houses of all are open and maintenance is freely supplied . . . The breadth of this Hercynian forest, which has been referred to above, is to a quick traveler, a journey of nine days. For it cannot be otherwise computed, nor are they acquainted with the measures of roads . . . It is certain that many kinds of wild beast are produced in it which have never been seen in other places.

Gallic War, VI, 22–28.

No real gods or priests, no property, no social order, no fields of corn for bread, no way of measuring distances, vast forests teeming with ferocious beasts, incessant intertribal warfare—barbarism indeed, and no prospect of Rome running the place at a profit.

But this isn't anthropology. It's politics. The whole point is to set up a contrast between the left bank of the Rhine (where Caesar has triumphed) and the right bank (which he has twice invaded with no success whatever). On *this* side are the Gauls: they farm in fertile fields; they worship proper gods who can be easily mapped onto the Graeco-Roman pantheon; they have basic laws, primitive elections, a social order of sorts, and their druids even write in Greek characters, sure proof of civilizable potential. Caesar has won for his people an entire country perfect for Romanization, and ripe for taxation. On *that* side of the Rhine, though, are the Germans.

At the same time, it's clear that the river isn't really the border between two entirely different cultures. Caesar tells us there's at least one tribe dwelling on the far side of the Rhine who were until recently Gauls in Gaul; vice versa, the Belgae, now living on the near side of the Rhine, have *sprung from the Germans only recently*. The Ubii, who live on the German bank of the Rhine, are steadfast allies of Rome, while on the Gaulish bank dwell hostile tribes, also apparently Germans. All through the *Gallic War*, people cross the Rhine to attack, to unite, to flee, or to migrate. Caesar himself used a German cavalry unit as an elite personal guard.

The reality along the banks of the Rhine in 58–53 BC seems to have been a fluid, baffling, and bloody mess, rather like today's Syria. But what kind of triumphal news would that be? So Caesar announces that he has discovered a natural boundary for Roman rule. The Rhine becomes a Roman version of the Sykes-Picot *line in the sand*, the border drawn arbitrarily through the Middle East by the British and the French after WWI. The peoples beyond the Rhine are declared irredeemably barbaric and their land a nightmarish wilderness. Worse, they are specifically hostile to Rome herself, *never refusing help to anyone who opposes the Romans.* Henceforth, Rome's mission is clear: keep a watch on the Rhine and give them hell every time they try to cross it.

Julius Caesar had invented the Germans.

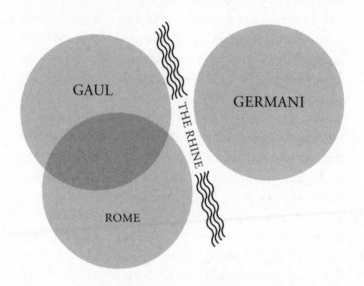

Gaul and Germany according to Caesar.

Germania Almost Becomes Roman

The Roman Republic, busy fighting itself and becoming an Empire after Caesar's murder, stuck to his line on the Rhine: civilizable Gauls *here*, Germans *there*. Of course, there were uses for uncivilized folk. The first Roman Emperor, Augustus, copied Julius Caesar in using a personal bodyguard of North-Rhineland Germans—as did Herod the Great, Rome's client King of Judea. In 17 BC, however, a large war pack of Germans crossed the Rhine, captured V Legion's holy symbol, its eagle, and took it back across the river in triumph. The brand-new Roman Empire could not permit its writ to be mocked like this, so it mobilized for its first great strategic offensive: the outright conquest of *Germania*.

The Emperor Augustus's younger stepson, Drusus, was given command. Jump-off points were built along the Rhine, giving birth to what are now Bonn, Mainz, Nijmegen, and Xanten. From these bases, Drusus led his legions and his navy from 12 BC–9 BC in an unbroken succession of victories the length and breadth of northwestern Germany.

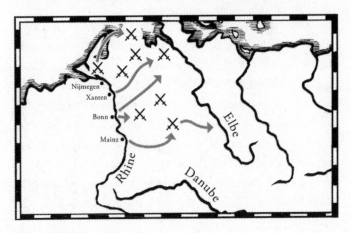

In 9 BC, Drusus reached the Elbe. There, according to the historians Cassius Dio and Suetonius, a vision of a gigantic female form advised him to turn back and cease his insatiable drive for conquests, for his days were numbered.

Drusus reaches the Elbe; wood engraving after Eduard Bendemann.

It's a seminal moment in the history of Germany and Europe. Stopping at the Elbe is not a normal military-political decision; it's one dictated by higher powers. Crossing the Rhine is fine; but the Elbe marks the end of reasonable ambition.

The final conquest of *Germania* between the Danube, the Rhine and the Elbe was slated for 6 AD. In perhaps the greatest single campaign ever planned by Rome, twelve legions—about 40% of the Empire's entire strength—were to envelop the last recalcitrant tribes in a vast pincer movement from the Rhine in the west and the Danube in the south.

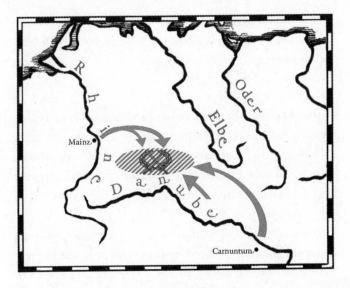

The Empire's grand plan, 6 AD.

Just a few days before the mighty offensive was due to begin, an auxiliary legion in modern-day Bosnia mutinied, sparking the *Great Illyrian Revolt* in the Balkans. The massed Rhine-Danube armies were hastily transferred south.

Back in *Germania*, despite the abandoned campaign, Romanization continued apace. Cassius Dio wrote that *cities were being founded. The barbarians were becoming used to holding markets, and were meeting in peaceful assemblies.* This sounds rather like Dick Cheney's idyllic dream of a post-Desert Storm Iraq, and traditionally it's been dismissed as gross exaggeration. Recently, though, archaeologists have found clear evidence that the Romans truly were constructing *Germania*. At Waldgirmes, 60 miles east of the Rhine, an entire military and civilian town complete with streets, a market, and a forum, has been uncovered. The coins found there date Roman occupation from 5 AD to 9 AD.

That second date was for many decades drilled into every German schoolchild's brain as the most memorable in German history.

Arminius and After

Rather like the British in India, the Romans in Germany found a patchwork of warring statelets and imposed upon it, for their own convenience, the notion of a single vast Nation. Like the British, they then created for this invented land a class of semi-acculturated leaders from whom they expected loyalty.

In 9 AD Publius Quinctilius Varus, governor of *Germania*, had spent the summer deep up-country, not at war but collecting taxes (with too heavy a hand, it was later said). On the way back to winter quarters on the Rhine, he made the mistake of trusting his Romanized table-companion, Arminius (the Latinized version of Hermann), the son of the chief of the northwestern Cherusci tribe, who'd been educated in Rome itself. Arminius told him that there was a small rebellion going on nearby, and that the Romans ought to show the flag there just one more time this year. Despite being warned by Arminius's own father-in-law not to trust him, Varus agreed and, convinced he was in fully pacified territory, set off without even bothering to organize his three legions into proper war-march formation. Camp followers and all, the Romans struck out into the narrow paths and dense forests which Caesar, fifty years before, had carefully avoided. There, they were wiped out in the ambush known as the *Battle of the Teutoburg Forest*, amid well-attested scenes of horror that would strain even today's moviemakers. Following a breakthrough by British amateur Major

Tony Clunn in 1985, archaeologists are now certain that the battlefield was at Kalkriese, in Lower Saxony.

Roman cavalry mask discovered at the Kalkriese site.

In the aftermath, almost every Roman foothold east of the Rhine was destroyed. It was a great defeat for Rome, but not the epochal turn that Lutheran and Prussian historians later invented. From 14 to 16 AD Drusus's son, Germanicus, ravaged the land in vengeance and finally managed to bring Arminius and his allies to bay on the banks of the River Weser. The eve of battle was the stuff of legend. Arminius and a brother who'd stayed loyal to Rome traded insults across the river—in Latin. Germanicus provided the model for Shakespeare's Henry V by touring his troops incognito in the darkness. Come the morning, the Germans were routed and slaughtered so that *ten miles were strewn with bodies and abandoned weapons* (Tacitus). Soon afterward, Arminius/Hermann, the first hero of German nationalism, was murdered in obscure circumstances by his fellow countrymen.

The Rhineland was secure again. The Roman army, like all armies, preferred tough boys from the backwoods to city youths, and the Germans now became their most-favored recruits. During the Roman conquest of Britannia, German troops swam the Thames in full armor to win the vital Battle of the Medway. The Imperial bodyguard itself was so thoroughly German-manned that it was known by the cowed citizens of Rome simply as the *cohors Germanorum*. In parts of the Rhineland, providing soldiers for Rome became the mainstay of the whole local economy.

Rome was now enjoying its greatest days—a near-century of exceptional peace, stability, and prosperity under the so-called *Five Good Emperors:* Nerva, Trajan, Hadrian, Antoninus Pius, and Marcus Aurelius—and moving inexorably forward on all fronts, including Germany. We've only recently discovered just how far. Around 20 AD, the Greek geographer Strabo had seen Germany thus:

Map of Europe according to Strabo.

The Romans, he wrote, *have not yet advanced into the parts that are beyond the Albis [Elbe]*. But by 150 AD, the great scholar of Alexandria, Ptolemy, had drawn *Magna Germania* extending far beyond it:

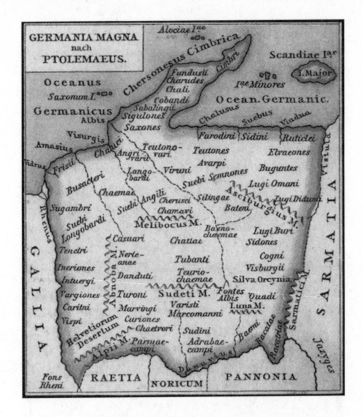

Until very recently, it was believed that much of Ptolemy's map was pure imagination. Then, in 2010, a team from Berlin Technical University, benefitting from a newly discovered version of the map and modern computing power, decided that it was far more accurate than had hitherto been believed—so accurate, in fact, that it could not possibly have been drawn by a man sitting in a library on the North African coast unless he had access to military-grade surveying information. The team concluded that by the early 2nd century AD, the Roman army must have thoroughly known the ground as far east as the Vistula, in today's Poland.

The Limes *That Lasted*

Although the Romans seem to have surveyed everything that would one day be called Germany, they never conquered anything like all of it. In fact, the future of Germany was largely dictated by precisely how far Rome truly ruled. There's no doubt how far that was, for the limit is still written unmistakeably in the soil.

The dates are vague, but by 100 AD at the latest the Romans were in full control of much of southwest Germany. By c. 160 AD they had formalized their rule by building the great fortified border, known as the *limes Germanicus*. This traced the Rhine, then cut eastward inland before following the River Main (to this day proverbial as the north-south divide in Germany) then heading south and east to modern-day Regensburg.

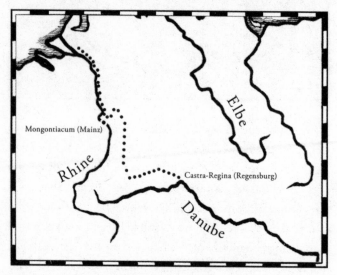

This fault line in German history is Europe's very own Great Wall: 350 miles long and with about a thousand forts or watchtowers, many still traceable. For years it was inexplicably ignored by historians, but in the last decade it has at last started to receive the attention it deserves. For the rest of this book we should remember exactly how much of Germany the Romans actually ruled.

If you lay the line of the *limes* over a map of modern Germany, it encompasses Cologne, Bonn, Mainz, Frankfurt, Stuttgart, Munich, and Vienna; just east of the line, places like Duisburg were originally Roman forward bases. In other words, all the greatest cities of the future Austria and West Germany except Hamburg grew up within, or in the immediate and daily shadow of, the Roman Empire.

The Noble Savage Germans

The most famous Roman account of the early Germans is the historian Tacitus's *Germania* (c. 103 AD). Like Caesar, Tacitus cast the Germans as the opposite of the Romans. But for him this was no bad thing, since he claimed the Romans had degenerated into a people made soft by vice and luxury, who merely groveled to their emperors. The Germans were barbarians, yes, but noble ones *uncorrupted by the temptations of public entertainments*.

Later patriots misread Tacitus's book as evidence that the Germans were never romanized. Actually, it means exactly the opposite. The Romans, like many later imperialists, liked nothing better than to read about wild and noble tribesmen on their frontiers—once they'd been beaten. If it took a real fight, so much the nobler all round. In 1745, all England trembled with fear as the Highland Scots invaded. No one thought them romantic. But once they'd been smashed at Culloden, the British Army almost immediately began using them as shock troops, and the English public fell in love with tales of their unspoiled, natural bravado. So it was with the Romans and Germans in 100 AD. The last serious rebellion in *Germania* had been in 69–70 AD, and that was only because Rome's crack German troops had felt insulted at the disbanding of the imperial bodyguard, the *cohors Germanorum*. Roman readers in Tacitus's day could safely enjoy tales of their very own wild *Germani*.

Tacitus's best-known, and most notorious, statement about the Germans is that they are a pure race *not mixed at all with other races* and all having the same physical appearance: blue eyes, red/blond hair, huge frames. Less often quoted is his insight into a central fact about *Germania*, right from its very beginnings. It is bounded to the north by the ocean, to the west by the Rhine and to the south by the Danube—but all that defines the boundary between the Germans and the scarcely known peoples to their east is *mutual fear*. Tacitus had hit on a great lever of German history: the uncertainty about how far east it actually stretched.

We'll come back to Tacitus later, when he is rediscovered in the 15th century AD. For now the important thing is that by c. 100 AD, despite the bloody setback of the Teutoburg Forest, Rome was in full control of the richest and most fertile parts of *Germania*.

The Beginning of the End

Roman troops returning from the Near East brought back a terrible souvenir. *The Antonine Plague*, possibly a smallpox pandemic, ravaged Western Europe between about 165 and 180 AD. Meanwhile, the Germans along the Danube came under pressure from more ferocious Germans, the Goths, who were expanding southward, and began to push against the undermanned Roman fortresses which hemmed them in.

With only plague-degraded legions at his disposal, the last of the *Five Good Emperors*, Marcus Aurelius, found himself obliged *to expose his person in eight winter campaigns on the frozen banks of the Danube, the severity of which was at last fatal to the weakness of his constitution* (Gibbon, *The Decline and Fall of the Roman Empire*). He was faced not with a single enemy, or a nation, but with a crazy political jigsaw puzzle, in which *Germani* was still just a catchall term for various tribes:

Roman *limes* and tribes of Magna Germania, around 160 AD.

Cassius Dio, *Roman History*, LXXII

Some of the tribes, under the leadership of Battarius, a boy twelve years old, promised an alliance; these received a gift of money. Others, like the Quadi, asked for peace, which was granted them. The right to attend the markets, however, was not granted to them, for fear that the

Iazyges and the Marcomani should mingle with them, and reconnoiter the Roman positions and purchase provisions . . . Both the Astingi and the Lacringi came to the assistance of Marcus, hoping to secure money and land. The Lacringi attacked the Astingi and won a decisive victory. As a result, the Astingi committed no further acts of hostility against the Romans . . . etc.

Marcus used a blend of sheer force and tempting offers to try to control things. After being defeated, selected Germans would be invited to become *foederati*, allies of Rome, who would fight against the other Germans in return for military aid and cash subsidies. At its core, this system depended on Rome's continuing ability to hand out a solid military thrashing now and then.

It eventually worked for Marcus Aurelius, though it killed him. But from the early 3rd century AD, Rome began to be challenged by the Persian Sassanid Empire for the huge wealth of the Near East. With resources diverted, it became harder and harder to control the German frontier.

In 235 AD the Roman armies on the Rhine mutinied and proclaimed a new kind of emperor, the gigantic and terrifying Maximinus Thrax, son of a Goth. The first emperor to be installed solely by the army and the first *altogether without literary education* (Gibbon) was half German. Maximinus was the beginning of the end for Rome. His reign opened the great *Crisis of the Third Century*, with some 20 different emperors in 49 years. By 284 AD, the lands beyond the Rhine and the Danube had been lost and a new *limes* had to be constructed along the riverbanks at vast expense. This line held for another century, but the Germans had *removed the veil that covered the feeble majesty of Italy* (Gibbon). From now on, Rome was purely on the defensive, and a purely defensive war only ever ends one way.

Darkness or Light?

We tend to think of civilized Rome going down at the hands of barbarian Germans, with the Dark Ages the sad result. But the lights were going out in Europe long before the Germans got to the switch.

After 235 AD, it was anybody's guess how long an emperor was going to last before being killed, or when the next civil war would devastate entire provinces. Just how different "Rome" had already become can be seen from the famous statue of the *Four Tetrarchs* (c. 300 AD); to us, it looks more like a set of Norse chessmen than a classical sculpture.

The Four Tetrarchs

A sort of order, which relegated Rome itself to the second city of the Empire after Constantinople, was restored by Constantine the Great (reign 306–337 AD), but only thanks to Germanic muscle. Constantine's first act on taking Rome in 312 AD was to abolish the legendary Praetorian Guard and replace them with the *Scholae Palatinae,* his own elite Germanic horse guards. The last great pagan Graeco-Roman thinkers, Libanius and Zosimus, both accused Constantine of conquering Roman civilization with an army of German barbarians. Constantine was Rome's first Christian emperor, so a military-political link between Germanic warlords and Roman Christianity was forged right from the start.

But even more massive change was coming, pushed, like

most really big things in history, by an epochal shift of populations.

The Wandering Germans

After 300 AD Germanic warbands seem to have been driven by some irresistible force to shift their habitations, in what's traditionally known as the *Völkerwanderungen*—the *Migrations of the Peoples*.

Since our only witnesses are Roman ones, we only know what they saw on their own borders. What was going on deep inside Germany is anyone's theory. Climate change is an obvious candidate, as is population growth or a simple desire for some of Rome's wealth. In some cases—such as that of the Goths, as we'll see—pressure from further east was certainly the cause. It's also been argued that the migrations were caused by the slow fall of the Roman Empire, and the resulting power-vacuum along its borders. But no one even really knows when it all started, let alone why. Marcus Aurelius's troubles back in the 2nd century may have been the very first sign. At any rate, the 19th-century map below shows why we can't even start to discuss in any detail what actually happened.

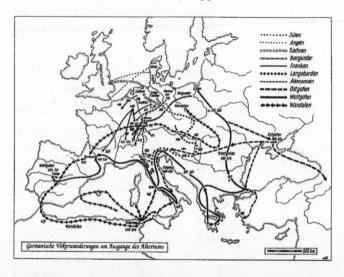

One thing we can say, though, is that the 19th-century image of entire tribes shifting (like the Boers or the pioneers of the American West) is misleading. The spectacular odysseys of these various Germans had almost no long-term effect on the linguistic map of continental Europe, a clear indication that the wanderers were overwhelmingly male. They might lord it over wretched farmers or unmilitary townsmen for a few generations; but without their own womenfolk, they would disappear almost without linguistic trace (language being normally transmitted down the maternal line) when they were finally defeated or simply absorbed. The native tongue would then resurface.

This happened all across Europe and North Africa. The only place where a literate, romanized, Christian culture was permanently obliterated by an entire new population of these illiterate, pagan Germans was in the lowland portion of the largest island of the archipelago northwest of the mouth of the Rhine, i.e. England. But that's another story.

As for the continental Germans, the first proper history we have belongs to the Goths.

The Goths—Saviors of Rome?

From teenage fashion to horror movies to architecture, the word *Gothic* has become a catchall title for anything dark, irrational, and anticlassical. The Goths would have been horrified.

True, they'd been the first barbarians ever to kill a Roman Emperor, but that had been back in the crisis-ridden days of the 3rd century, in 251 AD. By the 4th century, they'd become the first Christian, literate Germans, and had even translated the Bible from Greek into Gothic. They were loyal Roman *foederati*, with *an hereditary attachment to the*

Imperial house of Constantine (Gibbon), and their destruction of Rome began with a desperate plea for asylum within it.

In 375 AD, the Huns appeared from the Eurasian Steppes, sending the Goths recoiling from modern-day Ukraine toward the Danube. They clamored to be allowed to cross the river, if only to settle in the most wretched parts of the empire they had served so well. The Romans, forced to choose between *admitting or rejecting an innumerable multitude of barbarians, who are driven by despair and hunger to solicit a settlement on the territories of civilized men* (Gibbon), found the worst possible solution. The Goths were ferried over the Danube, but under conditions so harsh that Rome's petitioners, starving and desperate, now began to wage war on the Empire from within it.

In 378 AD, they killed the Emperor Valens and routed his army at Adrianople, in today's Turkey, becoming the real king-makers of the Empire. When the Visigoths under Alaric sacked Rome in 410 AD, it was just grand collateral damage in a war among Romano-Germans: Alaric's main opponent, Stilicho, was a Vandal from modern-day Austria. For the final twenty ghostly years of its existence after Rome was again sacked in 455 AD, the Western Empire was ruled, *de facto* if not *de jure*, by the half-Visigoth warlord Ricimer, who appointed and killed off Emperors as if they were minor diplomats. It was finally abolished by Odoacer, who may or may not have been some kind of German, in 476 AD. From then until 800 AD, *the Roman Empire* meant only the Eastern Empire centered on Constantinople (aka Byzantium).

Odoacer was himself personally killed in 493 AD by the most Roman of all Goths, Theodoric the Great (454–526 AD). Theoretically in the service of the Emperor, Theodoric became in

practice his full equal, and independent ruler of Italy. From his seat at Ravenna, he gave Italy something it had not experienced since Constantine two centuries earlier: thirty years of stable rule and virtually complete peace. His extraordinary tomb (left) still stands whole at Ravenna, looking like some apprentice classical architect's contribution to the Maginot Line. Its roof, incredibly, is a single slab of limestone weighing 300 tons.

Below are two coins minted around 500 AD. One was made for Zeno, the Roman Emperor (i.e. of the surviving, eastern half of the Empire), the other for his notional subordinate Theodoric, King of the Goths and ruler of Italy. Both were palace-dwelling, law-giving, church-building Christians.

The Gothic coin on the right is not that of a barbarian, the Roman one on the left nothing like those of Hadrian's day. The decline and fall of Rome had more or less intersected with the rise of the Germans.

In 235 AD the various Germans had been illiterate barbarians trapped in Germany by Roman power. By Theodoric's death in 526 AD, they were muscular Christians who controlled the entire former Western Empire.

The most successful of them, as it turned out, were the ones who stayed in their old homeland of romanized *Germania*. They would outlast the Vandals, Visigoths, Lombards, and Ostrogoths, reboot European civilization and give their name to a great nation. But it wasn't Germany.

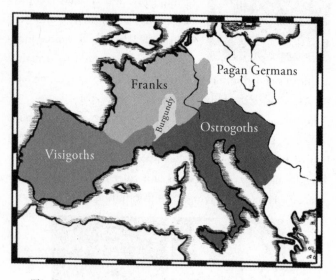

The Germanic Kingdoms at the death of Theodoric, 526 AD.

PART TWO

The Second Half-Millennium
526 AD–983 AD

The Germans Restore Rome

The Heirs of Rome

The Franks enter history in 297 AD, when they forced their way across the Rhine into modern Holland/Belgium. Rome tolerated their presence there, and by the middle of the 4th century AD they had become loyal *foederati* of the Empire. There's a famous inscription from Aquincum (Budapest) from this period, which nicely expresses who this man thought he was: *Francus ego, civis Romanus, miles in armis* (*A Frank am I, a Roman citizen, a soldier in the army*).

When the nomadic cavalry hordes devastated Europe from the southeast in the 4th and 5th centuries, geography was, as usual, fate. The Franks dwelled far enough to the northwest to escape the main impact. They were able to survive the meltdown of the southern European economy because they were heavily involved in sea-trade with Britain and Scandinavia. Long experience with the Roman army had taught them how to fortify their lands with *castres* and deflect their wandering cousins toward easier targets. So, uniquely, the Franks didn't take part in the great migrations. They stayed put in their own lands, where their military elite had long spoken Latin as well as German. From this uniquely secure bicultural base, they were able to expand slowly south and west amidst the chaos, until their royal line entered history as the Merovingians.

What the Merovingians felt about themselves is clear from the tomb of the dynasty's founder, Childerich I (died c. 482 AD). When it was discovered in 1653, his bones were still visibly arrayed in a Roman military commander's cloak and he had been provided with money for the afterlife in the form of coins going back to the Roman Republic. As far as the first Merovingian and his mourners were concerned, he died a military prince of the Roman Empire. In 486 AD, his son Clovis defeated the last rival force claiming to represent the Western Empire, before himself converting to Christianity (496 AD). The theoretical end of the Roman Empire meant next to nothing in the Rhineland.

When the power of the Goths was broken forever (though at the cost of exhausting the Empire itself) in the Gothic Wars (535–554 AD), the Merovingians were the great ben-eficiaries. They spent the 7th century securing what's now France, but as far as German history goes, the vital thing is that they never lost or abandoned their ancestral power base straddling the Rhine, which was no more a real cultural border in 700 AD than it had been in 58 BC. They ran their Franco-German empire through Latin codices that mixed tribal Germanic laws with the Roman legal heritage.

In 732 AD they became the saviors of Western civilization. The seemingly invincible, hyper-modern state-cum-religion, Islam, was advancing up through Spain and into France in the shape of the Ummayad Caliphate, but was stopped forever at the *Battle of Tours*. It wasn't a king who defeated the Muslim armies, though, for the late Merovingian kings were notoriously feeble, and real power was wielded by their chief servants. The hero of 732 AD was the unheroically-titled Mayor of the Palace, Karl Martell.

Martell's son, Pepin, did away with the fiction of Merovin-gian power and founded his own Frankish dynasty in 751 AD. As a usurper, Pepin needed legitimacy, fast—and the Papacy needed a powerful friend to help it regain Roman independence from Constantinople. In 753 AD, Stephen II became the first Pope ever to journey north of the Alps. Pepin committed the Franks to defending the Papacy and gifted lands for Roman Popes to rule as their own in the *donation of Pepin*. In return Stephen personally and publicly anointed Pepin and his two sons with holy oil in a mighty ceremony at Saint-Denis in January 754 AD.

This deal between the Roman Church and Frankish power was the blueprint for the coming centuries: the warlords handed some of their actual, earthly power and wealth to the Church; the Church then declared them to be more than mere warlords. Power-sharing on this model could still be seen at work in Europe until well within living memory, in Franco's Spain or De Valera's Ireland.

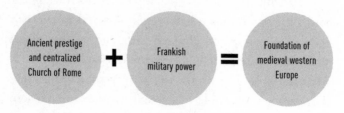

Ancient prestige and centralized Church of Rome **+** Frankish military power **=** Foundation of medieval western Europe

The Deal of Saint-Denis, 754 AD.

The lights were going on again in Western Europe. One of the two boys blessed at Saint-Denis by Pope Stephen was to loom so large for so many generations that until 1971 the British used the monetary system he laid down and, to this day, in Slavic languages bordering Germany to the east, as well as in Hungarian, the very word for *king* comes from his name: Karl the Great, better known as Charlemagne.

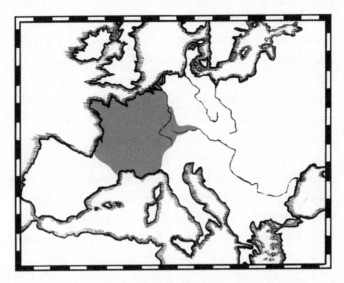

The great continuity: Roman Gaul and Germania, c. 160 AD . . .

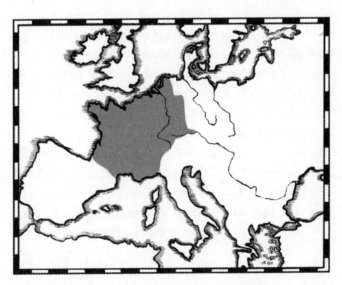

. . . and the Frankish Kingdom in 768 AD, at Charlemagne's accession.

The Vital Continuity

Charlemagne's memory is so enduring because he was the bridge that finally ensured that the culture of Roman Europe was transported into the medieval world, and hence to us.

He inherited a kingdom that covered almost exactly the same area as the combined Gaul and *Germania* ruled by Rome at the height of its power some 500 years earlier.

As a Frank, he came from a long-recognized cultural group called (by other people) *the Germans* and spoke a West Germanic language. But whatever the tongue of his birth, he worked tirelessly to ensure that Latin was taught throughout his multiethnic realms, using textbooks he personally commissioned, as the language of law, government, and worship.

The *Carolingian Renaissance* was the culmination of a vital continuity, meaning that Germans living within or near the Roman *limes* never really experienced an interruption to rule by Rome-facing elites. Whether these elites were pagan Romans, the Christianized *foederati* of the later Empire, or Christian Merovingians and Franks, they all looked to the Roman Empire as the legal, religious, and diplomatic source. The Rhine-Danube super-region of Germany always remained coupled to Western Europe.

In fact, the great dilemma facing Charlemagne at his accession was a thoroughly Roman one: what to do about the un-romanized, pagan Germans bordering his empire to the east? Here they are, described by Charlemagne's biographer, Einhard (who evidently doesn't see himself as one of them):

> The Saxons, like almost all the tribes of Germany, were a fierce people, given to the worship of devils, and hostile

to our religion, and did not consider it dishonorable to transgress and violate all law, human and divine.

After thirty years of vicious fighting, several thousand executions and the threat (issued in 785 AD) that refusing baptism would henceforth be a capital crime, Charlemagne eventually managed what the Romans hadn't, quelling, converting, and ruling all the Germans up to the river Elbe. He was now ready for the greatest step of all.

Rome, Restored—and Germany, Doomed?

On Christmas day, 800 AD, Charlemagne was crowned Roman Emperor, publicly adored and acclaimed by Pope Leo III as *imperator* and *augustus*. All over the continent, the coronation was seen as a restoration, and Charlemagne's capital, Aachen, was called the new Rome. His official seal said it plainly: *Renovatio Romani Imperii (Renewal of the Roman Empire)*. The coins struck in the name of *Karolus Imp Aug* were consciously modeled on the long-gone days of Rome's true greatness: he doesn't stare out at us like some coroneted Late Roman emperor, but is shown laurel-wreathed and clean shaven, in classical profile:

The Western Empire was back, and western Germany was its seat of power. When Charlemagne laid down the eastern boundary between his empire and the pagans to the east, he even used the Roman name for his border: the *limes*.

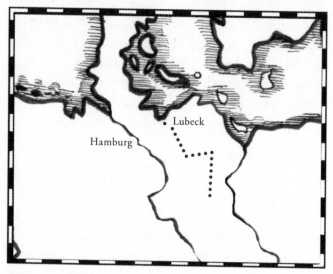

The Limes Saxoniae, early 9th century. It's almost identical to the East German border here in the mid-20th century.

There was now a German sitting on the throne of the Caesars and ruling all Western Europe from a German city. Yet paradoxically, German culture was facing extinction.

Charlemagne's empire ruled, judged, and worshipped in Latin. We know very little of the German language he presumably spoke in private, though we do know he ordered a now lost collection of its myths and tales.

Recorded German, c. 800 AD

Almost all we know is from religious words and fragments translated from Latin, plus a few magic charms and a wonderful two-page fragment of epic poetry, the *Hildebrandslied*, which tells how Fate set a father and son to fight in opposing armies. The most striking relics are the small collections of useful everyday phrases (the so-called *glosses*) set down with Latin translations in the margins of Latin religious texts. Just as in modern guide books, these were meant as a quick aid for educated travelers who might need to give orders to (or insult) the non-Latin speaking lower orders: *skir minen part* (shear my beard); *gimer min suarda* (gimme my sword); *vndes ars in tino naso* (hound's arse in thine nose).

The word that became *deutsch* wasn't originally anything to do with Germany. Charlemagne's chaplain wrote in 786 AD that in England, church business was conducted in both Latin and *theodisce* (meaning the language of the people, in this case Anglo-Saxon). Later, *theodisce* was used to mean the non-Latinate Frankish tongues, and eventually became *Deutsch/Dutch*.

Now, on the eastern borders of that empire, a great new people arrived on the European scene: the Slavs. No one quite knows when or where the *Slav Ethnogenesis* happened (patriotic Russian, Ukrainian, and Polish historians all lay claim to it), but by 800 AD they had occupied the lands up to the Elbe and even beyond it.

At Charlemagne's death in 814 AD, the place the Romans in 150 AD had called Magna Germania—Greater Germany—was entirely partitioned between the renascent Latin-ruled empire based in the Rhineland and the Slavs advancing from the east.

If Charlemagne's multiethnic, Latin-ruled empire had held together for another few generations, it's altogether possible that Frankish German culture might have followed its cousins, the once-mighty Goths and Vandals, into the dusty book stacks of history.

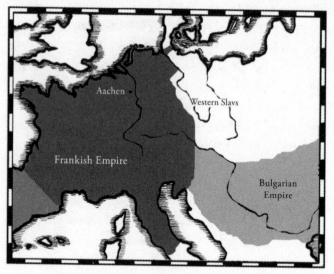

No space for the Germans: Europe in 814 AD.

The Birth of Deutschland

Instead, things after Charlemagne's death turned into a 30-year-long episode of *A Game of Thrones*: a wild dance of uprisings, alliances, usurpations, restorations, family feuds, solemn vows and blatant oath-breakings, in which the great empire broke up into the national outlines of modern Europe.

In 842 AD two of Charlemagne's warring grandsons, Louis the German (who held sway east of the Rhine) and Charles the Bald (who ran what is now France) came to Strasbourg with their armies to do a deal against their other brother, Lothair. This meeting was so important that it wasn't enough for the brothers and their elite advisers (who could all speak Latin, naturally) to do a deal amongst themselves. Each of them needed all his supporters to hear exactly what was being promised. But there was a problem: the ordinary men from West

Francia and East Francia couldn't understand each other. The peoples west and east of the Rhine, officially divided by Julius Caesar, were by now genuinely different. The only solution was for Charles and Louis to come to terms in Latin, then for their scribes to make West Frankish and East Frankish translations of the agreement and finally—in what's surely one of the greatest tableaux in European history—for each to read out the memorandum personally, in the language of his brother's army, in front of everybody. These *Strasbourg Oaths* are gold dust for historians of language: on this single day, French first appears as a recorded tongue and German attains the rank of a diplomatic language.

The Strasbourg Oaths, 842 AD

Each oath begins "For the love of God and for the Christian people . . ."

Louis the German (to Charles's West Frankish army): *Pro Deo amur et pro christian poblo . . .*

Charles the Bald (to Louis's East Frankish army): *In godes minna ind in thes christianes folches . . .*

A year later, the *Treaty of Verdun* (843 AD) divided the empire between Charlemagne's three surviving grandsons, Charles, Louis, and Lothair.

Now, at the very birth of Germany in any modern sense, the conundrum described by Tacitus came home to roost. Anyone could see where Louis's realm began—along the Rhine, of course—but where exactly did it end? Nobody knew. The Treaty of Verdun simply assigned Louis everything beyond the Rhine (ultra rhenum omnes). But did this everything stop at the Elbe, where the Germans themselves stopped? Or did it include the regions beyond the Elbe, which had done homage to Charlemagne, but never been conquered by him?

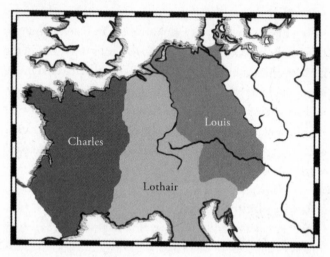

The Saxon Takeover

In 870 AD, Louis and Charles partitioned Lothair's realm between them, creating the West Frankish and East Frankish kingdoms which would become France and Germany respectively. Lothair's realm was left only as a name—*Lotharingia*—and as the memory of a thoroughly mixed Franco/German/Roman realm, a sort of gigantic Luxembourg covering much of modern Holland, Belgium, the Rhineland, Alsace, Switzerland, and northern Italy, to tempt future statesmen like Napoleon and the fathers of the EU.

The Elbe now became to the East Franks (we'll call them the Germans from now on, though nobody did at the time) what the Rhine had been to Caesar. It was a border you might be tempted to cross, but where the first priority was simply to hold against troublesome barbarians. The later

Carolingian kings (876–911 AD) had to spend most of their energy campaigning along the Elbe just to stop the pagan Slavs making incursions and keep them delivering tribute. The region was so undeveloped that this tribute was often calculated not in money, but in honey.

At this point, northern and eastern Europe were hit by the perfect storm that was the first half of the 10th century. Whether by coincidence or not, two almost supernaturally mobile pagan threats assaulted Germany just as a historic peak in volcanic plume activity ruined the harvests year after year. For a lifetime and more, Viking longships ravaged the North Sea coast and down the Rhine, while Magyar horsemen pillaged deep into southeastern Germany. This fatally undermined the last Carolingian, Louis the Child (aka Louis III, also aka Louis IV, which shows how confused things had become). The Germans were now desperate for a strong ruler focused on Germany. It was no good having a dynasty, no matter how prestigious, which was constantly subdividing its inheritance and always had half an eye on the glories of Rome.

When Louis died in 911 AD, the regional magnates of Germany did something which was to make the German throne unique in Western Europe: they abandoned the principle of descent and went back to the ancient Germanic practice of electing kings. They chose Conrad, Duke of Franconia, who had only the most distant maternal link to the Carolingian dynasty.

From now on, the history of the German throne is one of a permanent battle between royalty and high nobility. Kings naturally wanted their own sons to inherit; but whenever a king got too powerful, or was too weak, the regional magnates would revive the idea that the German throne was really an elective one.

Conrad died in 918, having been unable to impose his royal will on his ex-peers; his elected successor was Henry the Fowler, Duke of Saxony (thus nicknamed because the keen hunter was allegedly fixing his bird trapping nets when the news of his election arrived). Henry had no interest in the Roman Empire—his own tribe had converted to Christianity a mere century ago—and every interest in keeping the eastern borders secure against the Slavs.

He concentrated his new powers on his own home turf, carefully preparing his defenses, his offensive capabilities, and his prestige. Holy relics, most famously the Spear of Destiny (the lance that allegedly pierced Jesus as he hung on the cross), were systematically transferred to Saxony; the Eastern March was studded with new, fortified towns such as Meissen. Overlordship right up to the Elbe was restored. As for the Magyars, he steadily built up a cavalry-centered army to counter their mounted horde, and roundly defeated them in 933 AD. Henry's victories gave him such muscle that he was able to force the nobility to elect his son, Otto.

All Germania between the Rhine, the Danube and the Elbe now had a sole ruler who was not a Frank and whose father had been king. Germany seemed to be on the royal road to nationhood.

The Age of Silver

The trouble was that German kings couldn't forget the memory of Charlemagne's imperial glory. Otto the Great (as he became known) was crowned at Aachen in 936 AD sitting upon Charlemagne's own stone throne, despite being completely unrelated to him. It was a sign of intent.

Before he could think about Rome, Otto had to deal with his eastern question. It's in his reign that the word *teutonicis* is first recorded north of the Alps, in court documents which distinguish between Otto's German subjects and the *sclavanis*. The Slavs responded in kind by coining the word *nemoy* (*non-speakers*) as their own word for all Germans. It stuck, in every Slavic language. Almost a thousand years after Drusus had been supernaturally advised to stop there, the Elbe was still the great dividing line between a Rome-facing *us* and a distinct *them* (or vice versa).

Otto soon established his sway even beyond the Elbe, founding the two new bishoprics of Havelberg and Brandenburg in 948 AD. A border fortress on the river known simply as the great castle (magado burga) became his religious-political-military capital, Magdeburg. The area between the rivers Elbe/Saale and Oder was divided into marches (a march was the European medieval term for a border area

Contested German/Slav lands c. 960 AD.

where the king's writ only partially ran, and where semi-independent marcher lords ruled in his name by military force). Together, these marches occupied an area extremely similar to the future East Germany.

Once he'd crushed the Magyars at the great Battle of Lech (955 AD), Otto's eastern borders were secure and he set his sights on the greatest prize of all: Charlemagne's Roman imperial crown.

But there was a problem. Medieval Europe was obsessed with legitimacy, because the notion of proper legal title was the one check to the rule of physical force. Otto needed to justify his claim to be the true Emperor. He was completely unrelated to Charlemagne, so blood wouldn't do it; nor could he claim to rule the same empire as Charlemagne, since he didn't control West Francia (France). So by what right was he Emperor? His courtiers and churchmen came up with a radical new idea that was to echo down the centuries: that there was a mysterious but profound connection between the crown of Germany and that of the historic Roman Empire. This vision was known as the *translatio imperii*.

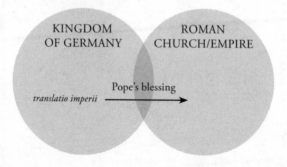

Otto duly became Roman Emperor in 962 AD and the trouble with the relationship became clear almost immediately.

The Papacy could legitimize and glorify your rule; it could help unite your vast domain; but in using the Pope like this, you tied yourself to defending him.

Otto, who had been all-powerful in Germany, now spent years on end away in Italy, buttressing his Pope by force of arms, while his control of his core lands weakened. His son, Otto II, was even more Rome-centric, and died there early, in 983 AD, leaving Otto III as merely an infant. Back on the marches of Germany, the peoples beyond the Elbe took their chance.

The *Great Slav Revolt* of 983 AD is as central to Slavic history as 9 AD is to German history. It was the event which guaranteed cultural survival. Just as the Romans lost everything beyond the Rhine in 9 AD, the Germans were thrown clean back across the Elbe in 983 AD. Within a few decades, the Poles and the once-dreaded Magyars (today: Hungarians) had founded independent Christian realms and structures, while the Bohemians (today: Czechs), initially subordinate to the Poles, were not far behind. These new kingdoms paid no tribute to German rulers and had their own direct lines to the Pope.

Suddenly, Europe was far bigger. Germany still ended exactly where Drusus and Germanicus had called a halt 1,000 years before, on the Elbe. Now, though, there were Christian realms all along its eastern borders. Germany was no longer at the edge of Europe, but at its heart.

How did Germany fit into this newly enlarged Europe? Did Rome decide what happened in all Europe, including in Germany? Or did German rulers—as Otto the Great had claimed—have a special relationship with the historical Roman Empire, making them the natural leaders of all Europe?

PART THREE

The Third Half-Millennium
983 AD–1525 AD

There Is a Battle for Germany

The Three-Way Fight

German history for the next six centuries is a three-way see-saw between kings, the nobility, and the Church. In some ways, it's the same pattern as in English or French history, but in Germany things were complicated (a) by the tradition of an elective rather than hereditary monarchy, and (b) by the fatal temptation for German kings to believe they were also Emperors of Rome.

King, Barons, Pope

The personnel changed, but the underlying drives remained the same over the centuries:

ALL KINGS: wanted to make the German throne heredi-tary and become Roman Emperor; needed to keep Nobles and Pope onside, but without yielding too much to them.

ALL NOBLES: wanted to elect kings strong enough to ensure order and defend Germany, but not strong enough to do away with elections.

ALL POPES: wanted strong Emperors who would pro-tect and need the Church, but not so strong they could control the Papacy.

At first, the new *Salian* dynasty, founded by the successful warlord Conrad II after the last *Ottonian* (Henry II) died child-less, seemed on the way to full control. Conrad's son, Henry III succeeded without trouble from the nobles and installed four obedient German Popes in a row. The crown was on top. In

1056, however, Henry committed that cardinal error for any medieval king: he died before his only son was out of infancy. With Henry IV still a child, everything was up for grabs again.

The German nobles jockeyed amongst themselves; the Slavs across the Elbe made a last, great mass return to paganism, killing their own converted king and besieging Hamburg. Eventually, Henry, by now an adult ruler, was able to restore peace along the Elbe frontier and come to terms with the nobility—only for the tough new Pope, Gregory VII, a veteran of Italian power-politics, to make his own move.

Gregory saw in Henry's troubles a chance to free the Papacy from German domination. Thanks to the Crown-Church deals that had been done since the early Carolingians, senior churchmen were often also high-ranking servants of the emperor, wielding great earthly powers. Gregory now declared that only the Pope could choose and invest them. This made the *Investiture Crisis* a major threat to royal power. Henry shot back that the Pope was only the Pope at all if the German king/Roman emperor said so. Gregory countered with his trump card. He excommunicated Henry, invalidating at a stroke any vows of loyalty his subjects had previously made to him.

Henry's power over his own nobles was too weak to survive this threat, so he undertook a desperate winter journey which went down in the iconography of the Middle Ages. In January 1077, with only his family and a small retinue, the King of Germany and Roman Emperor crossed the

Henry IV begs the owner of Canossa, Mathilde, to intercede for him with Pope Gregory VII.

snowbound Alps into Italy, where he spent three days standing barefoot in a hair shirt before the castle of Canossa, until Pope Gregory finally relented and received him back into the Church.

It was only a pause for breath. The Pope backed the nobles in rebelling again; Henry invaded Italy and ended up at war with his own son; anti-Popes and anti-Kings were announced with alarming regularity. Eventually, both sides realized it couldn't go on. In the great *Concordat of Worms* (1122) the Papacy and the Empire tried to plaster things over with newly invented symbols and theatrical instructions for how, and by whom, bishops should be invested. The only real winners were the great nobles and churchmen of Germany, who took advantage of the decades-long impasse to strengthen their own independence from King or Pope.

The Wendish Crusade

There was one thing that the German nobles, the King/Emperor, and the Pope could all agree on: a crusade. And there was a handy one to be had right next door.

By the early 12th century, the climate of Europe had changed significantly from the bad old days of the early 10th. Whatever we nowadays think of global warming, the *Medieval Warm Period* (c. 950–1300) was an unadulterated boon to the farmers of Northern Europe, and the population of advanced regions was exploding. *East Elbia* (*Ostelbien*), the no-man's-land beyond the Elbe, neither German nor Polish, inhabited by tribes of Slavic pagans collectively known as the *Wends*, had always been a harsh, cold, marginal place of marshes, forests, and rivers. Longer growing seasons now made all that land tempting, and the German nobles were already nibbling away at it.

In 1147, the Pope and his trusted advisor Bernard (later Saint Bernard), Abbot of Clairvaux, formally declared the *Wendish Crusade*. The Church intended total war: the pagan *agents of the devil* were to be *subjugated* to the Christian religion (contradicting the usual doctrine that conversion had to be by free will) and the battle, wrote St. Bernard, was not to be stopped until *either their rites or the nations themselves had been wiped out.*

Things didn't go according to plan. The pagans resisted so forcefully that the German crusaders began to accept even the most superficial evidence of conversion, such as crosses hastily displayed on the battlements of besieged fortresses. The Pope's observers reported back with outrage to Rome that the German nobles were pursuing their own agenda of feudal conquest and tribute, not following the Church's more radical brief. Rather than becoming the clean sweep St. Bernard had envisaged, the conquest of East Elbia broke up into a series of ad hoc deals with local leaders.

The incompleteness of the German victory beyond the Elbe was to have a profound effect on the region's future. Although many land-hungry Germans now settled in East Elbia, the old Slavic inhabitants, with their language and culture, survived in pockets throughout the region. They were a constant reminder, generation after generation, that this was colonial land, taken by force from someone else who was still around and might one day fight back.*

---

* When a place is rural and colonial, fears and enmities, retold by the old to the young, easily leap the centuries. In deepest southern Ireland in the 1980s, a Catholic small farmer pointed out to me, with genuine bitterness, a large Protestant house that stood on land that was, he claimed, rightfully his family's. It sounded as though he was talking about some robbery or fraud in, perhaps, his father's lifetime. The house in question was of the mid-18th century.

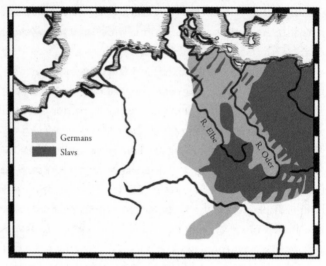

The settlement of the East c. 1200.

Even today, descendants of the Wends, known as Sorbs, dwell just north of Dresden.

The settlers developed—presumably for defense—a distinctive way of arranging their dwellings in circular form with an access track.

These round villages (*Rundlings*) are so distinctive that any German archaeologist can spot the signs of them in an aerial photo of a random German village or town, and immediately tell you that it lies east of the Elbe. Likewise, any German geographer can tell that if your hometown ends in -*in* (like Berl*in*) you very probably live east of the Elbe; if it ends in -*ow*, or -*itz*, you almost certainly do.

This brand-new, colonial Germany was to stay forever a palpably different place to the Germany which had already existed as part of Western Europe for 1,000 years.

The Golden Age

For the time being, however, things had never been better. When Friedrich I (known as *Barbarossa*) was elected King in 1152, he chose, like so many before and after him, to go for the Imperial crown. But he accepted what was essentially a dual monarchy. While he attended to the Empire in Italy and Sicily, he allowed his cousin, Henry the Lion, who'd grown mighty during the Wendish Crusade, to function as *de facto* ruler of Germany.

This power-sharing solution worked. The era seemed so uniquely fine to those who came after that, in the German imagination, Barbarossa became like King Arthur to the Britons: the great lord of a golden age who would one day rise again from his sleep within the Kyffhäuser mountains, in Germany's hour of need.

Under Barbarossa's son, Henry VI, new heights of imperial glory were reached. Henry's most famous coup was capturing Richard the Lionheart in 1193 and forcing him to acknowledge the emperor as feudal lord even of England. His early death in 1197, however, swung things back to the German magnates, and they now set in stone the ancient system of electing kings.

Henceforth, only the seven most powerful lords and archbishops would have a vote. These seven became known as the Prince-Electors, and they remained central to German history for the next half-millennium. Three were high Churchmen— the Archbishops of Mainz, Trier, and Cologne—who all also held the imperial rank of Arch-Chancellor. The other four were lay powers: the King of Bohemia (the Arch-Cupbearer), the Count Palatine of the Rhine (the Arch-Steward) the Duke of Saxony (the Arch-Marshall) and the Margrave of Brandenburg (the

The seven Prince-electors and their coats of arms. The three Churchmen wear caps.

Arch-Chamberlain).The three Churchmen were all based within the old Roman limes. Of the four worldly Electors, however, three had power bases on, or even beyond, the borders of Germany proper.

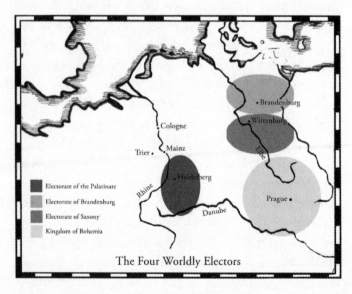

Electorate of the Palatinate
Electorate of Brandenburg
Electorate of Saxony
Kingdom of Bohemia

The Four Worldly Electors

Frederick II, whom they now elected unopposed, seemed the height of power and glory. He even liberated Jerusalem for

Christianity without a fight in 1229. Emperor, King of Germany, of Lombardy, of Sicily, of Burgundy, and of Jerusalem: *stupor mundi*, so was he hymned, *the wonder of the world*. But though he was awash with titles, his core power north of the Alps was really dependent on the Electors, and in 1231 they made him sign the *Privilege of Worms*, confirming their right to rule over their own lands.

The Magdeburg Horseman (c. 1240): the first, full, free-standing equestrian statue in Europe since the fall of the Roman Empire.

The great nobles now seemed rulers of the German roost, with the Emperor a splendid but distant figurehead. The arrangement seemed to work, for this truly was a golden age in Germany. The country was the very heart of Europe. It was economically booming, studded with masterpieces of late Romanesque architecture and producing sculptural and pictorial artifacts that could vie with the finest of any civilization. And almost overnight, it bore the most varied and splendid literature in all Europe, which now flowered in three very different forms.

Minnesingers

The Minnesingers (love singers) were aristocratic minstrels who followed the cutting-edge example of the French troubadours in producing delicate, short, formal love poems filled with nightingales, broken hearts, and almost religious (not to mention, sacrilegious) images of erotic devotion. These are still charming today.

The "Folk Epic"—The Saga of the Nibelungs

The ancient folk tales of the Germans had become mixed up with the great historical events of the *Völkerwanderungen* to include figures like Attila and Theoderic. In the grand blossoming of the late 12th/early 13th centuries, these tales were given literary form in the mighty *Nibelungenlied* (Saga of the Nibelungs). The German equivalent of the *Iliad*, it tells how the invincible warrior, Siegfried, is tamed by courtly love, only to be betrayed by courtly intrigue. After his death, the Germans are lured east across the Danube, where they are wiped out by Attila's Huns in an epic last stand, with no Christian consolation whatever.

The Courtly Epic

This form was derived from the latest French versions of the Arthurian tales, with long descriptions of the glories of courtly life and strange, semireligious, semierotic quests, tests and missions—for the Grail, for Love, for Purity. The most famous are the ones used later by Richard Wagner as the bases for vast operas: *Tristan und Isolde* and *Parzival*.

The dynamism and confidence of Germany in this age is best shown by the rise of two very different, though allied, groups of adventurers: the Teutonic Knights and the Hansa.

The Teutonic Knights Become Prussians

Beyond Christian Poland lived the *Pruscie*. Like the word *Germani*, coined almost thirteen centuries earlier, *Pruscie* was a Latin catchall name for various barbarian tribes. These were pagan Balts living in the lands roughly between modern Gdansk and modern Riga, and they were proving impossible for the young Polish kingdom to handle.

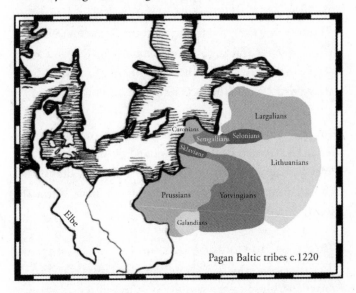

Pagan Baltic tribes c.1220

In 1226, Emperor Frederick II signed one of the central documents in the history of northeastern Europe: the *Golden Bull of Rimini* (so called because the metal seals used on it were of pure gold).

The Bull was for the Teutonic Order, originally merchants from Lübeck and Bremen who'd set off to tend wounded crusaders in the Holy Land. It invited them to militarize themselves and conquer the *Pruscie*. If they succeeded *where many others had failed*, they would be allowed to rule there, subject only to the emperor himself.

As illiterate, pagan barbarians rather than a Christian people, the *Pruscie* had no rights. In fact, the way the Teutonic Order described them calls to mind the way Caesar had described the *Germani* thirteen centuries before.

The Chronicle of Prussia, by Nicolaus von Jersoschin, c. 1320 AD

Because God was unknown to them, this gave rise to the error of foolishly worshipping every creature as god. Thunder, stars and moon, birds, animals, and even toads . . . Spawn of the devil who have no belief in God . . . when they have guests, they do the best for them that they possibly can (this is their greatest virtue).

The Teutonic Knights soon went far beyond the lands specified in the Golden Bull of Rimini and far beyond what the Poles had asked for. In 1266 the great English monk and scholar, Roger Bacon, complained about their distinctly worldly ambitions.

Roger Bacon Complains, 1266

In Prussia and the lands bordering Germany, the Templars and Hospitallers and the brothers of the Teutonic Order much disturb the conversion of infidels because of the wars which they are always starting, and because of the fact that they wish to dominate them absolutely. . . The pagan race has many times been ready to receive the faith in peace after preaching, but those of the Teutonic Order do not wish to allow this, because they wish to subjugate them and reduce them to slavery.

The result was the *State of the Teutonic Knights*, a heavily (but never completely) Germanized area east of Christian Poland, physically and politically unconnected to the rest of Germany. The knights' formidable HQ at Marienburg became the largest castle on earth. They had genuine, pagan tribes to battle against until 1413, and adventure-thirsty nobles from all over Europe came to help. In Chaucer's *Canterbury Tales* (1380–1400), the *parfit gentil knyght* has crusaded in *Pruce*. Over time the knights came to be known by the name of the very pagans they were extirpating, and a brand new sub-nation of Germans beyond Germany was born: the Prussians.

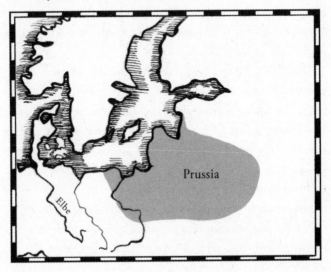

They went hand-in-armored-glove with their entirely un-chivalric compatriots in the Hanseatic League.

The Hansa: Legends of the Free Market

The German Hansa was a league of merchant towns with two main centers of gravity. Cologne ran trade with England and the Low Countries, while Lübeck controlled the Baltic operation.

In the Baltic, the link between the Hansa and the Teutonic Order was umbilical, and the Grand Master of the Order was the only non-merchant at the Hansa's board meetings.

Together, the Hansa merchants and colonizing knights had monopoly access to the treasures of northeastern Europe's wild frontierlands: furs, amber, tar, endless supplies of herring from the now-warmer Baltic, Swedish ore, and Russian timber for booming Western Europe. This was the last interface in the known world between a modern, money economy and illiterate, pagan hunter-gatherers: a canny Hansa merchant, protected by fear of the ruthless Order, could make a killing here.

The Hansa became so wealthy that it could loan, bribe, and lobby even large states like Henry IV's England into giving it tax breaks, monopolies, and quasi-sovereign enclaves. Englishmen called the Hansa merchants *Easterlings*, and their name came to stand for a reliable pound's-worth of money: the Pound *Sterling*.

If you crossed the Hansa, it could project physical force in a way the greatest modern corporation could only dream of. In 1368 it declared war on Norway and Denmark, and won. No non-state body has ever wielded such power in Europe.

The Electors, Triumphant

The Teutonic Order and the Hansa were not without their opponents, of course. But they flourished so greatly on Europe's northern fringe because the states which might have challenged them were hit by the most fearsome of all invaders from the southeast: the Mongol Horde under Batu Khan, grandson of Genghis Khan.

In 1241, the Mongols, having already traumatized Russia (forever, say many historians), swept in across the Great European Plain to within 40 miles of the present-day German-Polish border. There, at the Battle of Legnica, they annihilated a combined Polish-German-Czech force before heading south to help destroy the Hungarians.

To Europeans north of the Alps, it felt like the end times. By the time Frederick II died in 1250, Germany was in a state of complete anarchy, with rival claimants to the throne promising everything to anyone who'd declare for them. In 1257, Richard, brother of Henry III of England, was elected after a vast campaign of bribery. This French-speaking English lord only visited his German realm a couple of times, never going beyond the Rhine, before he died in 1272, a wretched captive of rival Anglo-Norman barons. By now, the German royal title was little more than a joke, and the Imperial throne had been vacant for decades.

The Electors, unchallenged in Germany, next chose as their king a man whom they assumed they would be able to control at will—a rather elderly German noble not even established enough to be an Elector himself. His name was Rudolph, Count of Habsburg, and he was already 55. It was an unspectacular arrival for the family who would come to be synonymous with the Empire, and whose various scions would decide much of European history until 1918.

Rudolph surprised everyone by disposing of his main rival, Ottokar of Bohemia, at one of the classic cavalry battles of the Middle Ages, *Marchfeld*, in 1278. But he never became emperor, and the Electors refused his son the throne: they were still the real power in Germany, and had no intention of choosing a king who might actually rule. The Habsburgs had arrived, but their day had not yet dawned.

The Electors were by now so confident atop the three-way seesaw of power that they were even ready to break the link between the Empire and the Papacy. In 1338 they declared that whoever they elected King of Germany was automatically *promoted to Emperor*—Pope or no Pope. The Electors had in effect declared that their votes (which they regularly sold for vast sums) were direct tools of the Divine Will.

Charles IV, who had amassed huge debts to buy those votes, tried to impose order on chaos with the *Golden Bull of Nuremberg* (1356), which soon became known simply as *the* Golden Bull, since it defined the constitution of the Holy Roman Empire until its dissolution in 1806. On the surface, it was all about the glory of the Emperor, and set out splendid theatrics for his coronation—*on horseback shall come the king of Bohemia, the arch-cupbearer, carrying in his hands a silver cup or goblet of the weight of twelve marks, etc.*—but the small print yielded all legal power to the Electors:

From the *Golden Bull,* 1356

Nothing now conceded or to be conceded in future by us or our successors the Roman emperors and kings . . . shall or may, in any way at all, derogate from the liberties, jurisdictions, rights, honors or dominions of the ecclesiastical and secular prince electors . . .

The royal-imperial power was now so small in practice that under Charles's incompetent son Wenceslaus (1378–1400), Germany again descended into chaos as the nobles machinated amongst themselves. In 1402, Rupert II was the last German king to try to gain the Imperial throne by sheer force of arms: he ran out of money halfway across the Alps, and his invading army melted ingloriously away.

By the start of the 15th century, centralized royalty on a French or English pattern seemed to be finished in Germany;

the future seemed far more likely to involve several entirely independent kingdoms, perhaps with a purely notional figurehead. What shifted power again was the unfinished struggle along the Elbe.

The Fifteenth Century: The Shadow of the East

At the start of the 15th century, German powers seemed in full control of the whole Elbe watershed and the Baltic coast. The Teutonic Knights seemed invincible in the north; Prague, the seat of the King of Bohemia, the premier Elector, was as much part of the German political scene as Cologne. Now, though, the Slavs pushed back.

Some argue that their chance came because the Black Death (1348–49) had taken a heavier toll among German incomers, who tended to dwell in tight-packed walled towns. At any rate, German domination was suddenly threatened.

In 1410, the new joint Kingdom of Poland-Lithuania shattered the power of the Teutonic Knights forever at Tannenberg. Among the warriors who fought alongside the Poles and Lithuanians was one John Trocznowski, also known as Jan Zizka (*one-eyed Jan*). After a stopover to help Henry V of England at Agincourt, Zizka became leader of a rebellion which posed a real threat to German dominance: the *Hussite* rising of the Czechs of Bohemia, under the banner of the reformer Jan Hus.

Hus attacked the privileges of the Roman clergy and is thus regarded as a forerunner of the Protestant Reformation, but this was really about the still unresolved battle between Slavs and Germans for control along the Elbe (or, as the Czechs called and call it, the *Labe*). Hus made Prague so unfriendly to thousands of German teachers and scholars that they left *en masse*, relegating the city's famous university to obscurity. After Hus was burned at the stake, his outraged followers, led by Ziska, rose up in rebellion in 1419. Skilled metal workers, they were the earliest adopters of field artillery. In an age when both horses and men were naturally gun-shy, their mobile cannon-waggons played havoc with aristocratic heavy cavalry. They defeated four separate Imperial crusades, repeatedly ravaged Saxony and Franconia, and even reached the Baltic coast, where (according to legend) they filled their drinking flasks with seawater to show that they, not the Germans, now owned it.

Eventually, the Hussites split and began fighting among themselves, enabling the Germans to recover. The wars ended in 1436, with a fudge which allowed the moderate Hussites to worship in their own way. But to three out of the four secular electors—the King of Bohemia, the Margrave of Brandenburg, and the Duke of Saxony-Wittenberg—this new Slavic pushback had been an existential threat to their core lands.

For once, they needed stability more than they feared a strong emperor. So when the Emperor Sigismund died in 1437, they rubber-stamped the seamless accession of his son-in-law, Albert II, followed by *Albert's nephew*, Frederick III. From now on, the notionally elected German King and Holy Roman Emperor was in practice a Habsburg. The Slavic resurgence had swung power back to the royal and imperial thrones, and given all Germany what looked like a natural ruling dynasty.

As Columbus set sail, west and south Germany was as indisputably a part of Western Europe as France or Italy. But the Elbe still marked a bitterly contested colonial frontier zone between Germans and Slavs, where the outcome was by no means certain.

Western Germany, which had existed for 1,400 years, and half-conquered East Elbia, only a few centuries old, were not growing together. On the contrary, the split was becoming more, not less palpable. The colonial, insecure nature of German East Elbia gave rise to a unique nobility known as the *Junkers*.

The Junkers and Their World

The name *Junkers* originally just meant *young lords*, because it was the younger sons of the German nobility who were ready to stake their lives on armed expansion into hostile East Elbia. They weren't a class but a caste, a warrior elite living in isolated strongholds on bleak land that was often marginal once again after the Little Ice Age replaced the Medieval Warm Period. Under *Gutsherrschaft* (*Landlord Rule*), a practice unique to East Elbia, they were virtually independent rulers on their estates, lording it over people who were not just dirt poor, but often cultural and religious foreigners (Poles, Balts, Russians). This remained so in East Prussia until within living memory. Since the Slavs were never completely conquered, the non-noble Germans in this colonial landscape ultimately depended on the Junker warlords for their defense and—like, say, the Poor Whites in the American South—developed a loyal servility to their masters, mixed with fearful scorn of the foreign underclass.

In the 15th century, the *Junkers* no more thought of themselves as *Germans* than anyone else did. But this was about to change—and in the crucible of that change, this essentially different sort of Germany, East Elbia, was to find an ideology of its very own.

The Reformation

On All Hallows' Day 1517, in the university town of Wittenberg on the Elbe, a prominent local priest who had (by his own account) recently had a mighty revelation while straining on the toilet, nailed a multi-bullet-point challenge to Rome onto the doors of the castle church. His name was Martin Luther and his *95 Theses* are regarded as the birth of the *Protestant Reformation*. As the words imply, it was at first a *protest* at certain usages of the Church, aiming merely to *reform* it.

Luther's thinking is based on two principles. The first, *sola scriptura (through scripture alone)* was the fundamentalist demand to cleanse the Church of everything that couldn't be based solely on the Bible. This was nothing new. St. Augustine himself could be (and often was) quoted in favor of it. Luther's own doctoral supervisor preached an Islamic-State-style eradication of all idolatrous images and shrines, however historic and beautiful. The second pillar of Luther's thought was the revelation which had come to him on the privy—*sola fide* (*by faith alone*). This was genuinely radical. He claimed that we cannot earn Heaven by confessing to a priest and doing penance, or even by boundless good works. We can only receive salvation as an unearned gift, directly from God, at the mystical instant we forget all earthly things, give up *the devil's whore, Reason*, and yield to true faith.

Together, these principles challenged the unique balance of Church and State power which had defined Western Europe since the deal between the Papacy and Charlemagne's father in 754 AD. It now split, bit by bit, into regions that remained loyal to Roman Catholicism, and those that developed various kinds of Protestantism (which often had very little in common other than that they denied the Pope's authority). We shouldn't confuse cause and effect, though. What made Luther's act so potent was not theology, but politics, for in 1517 the old game between the Electors, the Papacy, and the German/Imperial crowns was at fever pitch.

The Habsburg Emperor Maximilian (reigned 1493–1519) ruled not only Spain, Holland, Luxembourg, large parts of France and southern Italy, but also most of the New World. By now, the breathtaking size and wealth of that New World was becoming clear. Maximilian was determined that his grandson Charles (1500–58), would succeed to everything. Other European rulers were desperate to foil this plan for virtual world hegemony: both Francis I of France and Henry VIII of England declared themselves rival candidates for the throne of Germany. The Electors knew that this time, they could hold out for truly stupendous kickbacks and concessions from the Habsburgs.

In this atmosphere of feverish calculation, Albrecht, the new Hohenzollern Duke of Brandenburg, took on huge debts from the Augsburg-based Fugger banking dynasty to buy the bishopric of Mainz. This landed him one of the seven Electorships and ensured that he would be in on the vast bribes certain to come. It so happened that Pope Leo X, who was required to rubber-stamp this new Cardinalcy, was also up to his credit limit with the Fuggers, having spent wildly on hiring Raphael, Leonardo, and Michelangelo to beautify Rome. Leo wanted to go even further, and build a new St Peter's. So in 1516, Leo, Albrecht and the Fuggers did a deal. Leo would confirm Albrecht's elevation, and they would go 50/50 on a great new money-making scheme.

A famed preacher, Johannes Tetzel, was employed to travel Albrecht's lands, selling extra potent sin-clearing certificates called *St Peter's Basilica Indulgences*. These allegedly cancelled the need for dead sinners to spend time in the cleansing fires of Purgatory before entering Heaven. A representative of the Fugger bank traveled everywhere with Tetzel, keeping close tabs on the cash box. In 1517 the sales team descended amidst fanfares on Albrecht's territories—one of which lay near Wittenberg on the Elbe, where Luther preached.

Luther was appalled at the sight of his Saxon flock flocking into Brandenburg to buy the new indulgences. Being a trained lawyer as well as a priest, he framed his attack with great care, in Latin naturally, mixing pious theological niceties with his trademark down-home waspishness ("they claim the soul flies out of purgatory the moment the money tinkles into the box"). None of the *95 Theses* explicitly says that purgatory is an invention, that the sale of indulgences is a money-making fraud, or that the Papacy itself is corrupt. But it's all implied for anyone with ears to hear.

Suddenly, here was a propagandist and wordsmith who could debate in Latin with the most learned theologians yet also talk to ordinary folk of *swine* and *farts*, of *women* and *wine*, and whose acolytes used the new medium of print to spread his words with unearthly speed.

If there's one thread that runs right through the *95 Theses*, it's money. Many of the theses talk quite literally about it, and many more use metaphors of wealth, treasure, earnings, payments, debts, penalties. Luther's language was right for the time, because his huge impact wasn't really about theology at all. Both in person and through his writings, he soon became a handy weapon in the ancient struggle to decide who truly ruled—and therefore, taxed—Germany.

The Reformation Becomes Political

In June 1519, the Electors decided they couldn't resist the vast bribes that Charles, backed by the mighty Fugger bank, offered them, and made him Charles V, King of Germany.

Life and Deeds of Charlemagne, Cologne 1521, showing him handing over to Charles V.

Beforehand, they had forced him into the so-called *Electoral Capitulation* which guaranteed that Germans would run Germany under him and that no foreign troops would be stationed there. But things were edgy, for Charles V ruled a vast world empire *on which the sun never sets* (the phrase was coined for his realms, not for the later British Empire). Here for once, was a king/emperor who had the power and wealth truly to become a new Charlemagne. Who knew whether Charles would keep his word to the German princes once he became Emperor?

To secure their position against a ruler with such unheard-of resources, the German nobility needed to find new reserves of their own. They had to enlist the support of non-noble Germans, by claiming that they were acting in the interests of the *nation*. This was a cutting-edge idea, first recorded in Germany after 1450, and only officially enshrined in 1512, when Maximilian referred to his realm as the *Holy Roman Empire of the German Nation* (*Heiliges Römisches Reich Teutscher Nation*).

Luther was the man to pick up this new idea and run with it. By 1520, he had started his epochal translation of the Bible into German. His rhymes and rhythms, consciously drawn from the speech of ordinary people, are timeless. Even the glories of the King James Bible in English can't compete: *the mills of God grind slowly* sounds fabulous when read aloud, but *Gottes Mühlen mahlen langsam* beats it every time. Luther now unleashed his incomparable new German pen on a *national* tale of historical victimhood.

> ### From "To the Christian Nobility of the German Nation" (1520)
> The Emperors Frederick, the First and the Second, and many other German emperors were, in former times, so piteously spurned and oppressed by the popes . . . Therefore let us rouse ourselves, fellow Germans, and fear God more than man, that we be not answerable for all the poor souls that are so miserably lost through the wicked, devilish government of the Romanists.

Luther and his supporters appealed to the recently rediscovered *Germania,* and cast themselves as Tacitus's *Germani*—that is, as lovers of simple freedom and manly virtue, the moral opposites of a luxurious and degenerate Rome. Luther himself, an educated churchman, was happy to claim kinship with the pagan chieftain who had dealt Rome such a blow in 9 AD: *In the chronicles* (said Luther in his so-called table talk) *we read of a certain Cheruscan prince, a man from the Harz called Hermann, who dealt the Romans a devastating defeat and killed 21,000 of them. Well, now Luther the Cheruscan, from the Harz, is laying waste to Rome!*

The attractions of loosening the tie with Rome, keeping the money in-house, controlling one's own church, and parceling up all that ecclesiastical land were as obvious to the German princes as to Henry VIII of England.

> Frederick, the Elector of Saxony, and the other princes who supported Luther saw the advantage of putting themselves in charge of the Church and its lands. They increased their own power at the expense of pope and emperor—and so Lutheranism was born.
>
> John Hirst, *The Shortest History of Europe*

But for the rulers of Germany, there was a danger, too. Might not Luther's fundamentalism radicalize their subjects into denying all earthly authority?

Luther was soon working on this problem. In 1522 he refused to support an uprising of poor nobles, even though it was led by men who considered themselves his supporters. He discovered biblical passages which, he claimed, said that all rulers were there by God's will. Since people now had a direct line to God and were saved by faith alone, they could, should and must leave politics entirely to the earthly authorities. The true Christian (he wrote, in *On Temporal Authority*, 1522) *submits most willingly to the rule of the sword, pays tax, honors those in authority, serves, helps, and does all he can to further the government.*

Three years later, the peasants revolted en masse, expecting Luther to support them. Instead, he went even further in backing the forces of law and order—whatever they might be, and however harshly they might act. In *Against the Thieving, Murderous Mob of Peasants* (1525), he wrote that the rebels were *faithless, perjured, disobedient, rebellious murderers, robbers, and blasphemers, whom even heathen rulers have the right and power to punish . . . they should be smashed, throttled, stabbed, in secret and openly, by anyone who can, just as one must kill a rabid dog.*

The peasants were duly massacred in their thousands, with reforming priests on hand to encourage and bless the princely troops. The Reformation—and the prospect of getting their hands on all that Church land and money—was now safe for the rulers of Germany.

The first to take the plunge were the furthest from Rome, the Teutonic Knights. Their Grand Master, Albrecht von Brandenburg-Ansbach, having met Luther personally, declared himself no longer the mere head of a Catholic Order, obedient to the Pope and Emperor, but the Protestant Duke of Prussia in his own right, notionally subservient only to the King of Poland.

This was on April 10, 1525. It's the most important date in German history between 800 AD and 1866. In that strange colony way beyond the Elbe, beyond even Poland, where genuine pagans had dwelled until scarcely a century before, there was now, for the first time since Charlemagne's conquest of the Saxons, a German realm which refused all allegiance to the church, or the emperor, of Rome.

Prussia and the political Reformation were born in the same moment, as a direct challenge to the great continuum of the West.

PART FOUR

The Fourth Half-Millennium
1525 AD–Present

Germany Goes Two Ways

Stalemate

Others followed where Prussia had gone and the newly Protestant princes now founded the *Schmalkaldic League* (1531), which only Lutheran rulers could join and which had its own standing army. The idea of a completely German, non-Roman Germany was gaining ground. But the League was still up against the mightiest ruler on Earth.

The Emperor Charles V, in the Titian he commissioned after Mühlberg. In fact, he was in such pain from gout that he had to be carried to the battlefield on a litter.

By 1543, Charles V had triumphed in his great struggle against France and seen off the high tide of the Ottoman Empire in Europe. He was now in no mood to compromise. In 1547, for the first time since 16 AD, foreign, armored, highly trained professional infantry—the dreaded Spanish *tercios*—marched across the Danube and deep into Germany under the flags of the Roman Empire and its religion, bent on final conquest. The decisive battle was won on the Elbe, at Mühlberg. Once again, a Roman Emperor stood victorious on that riverbank, and seemed to bestride Germania.

However much the grandees of Germany disliked one another, they disliked the prospect of losing their unique privileges even more. They banded together, Protestant and Catholic, and told Charles they would call on help from the French rather than allow him to rule absolutely. Charles eventually conceded the *Peace of Augsburg* (1555), which declared that it was up to each German ruler, great or small, to choose:

cuius regio, eius religio (*whoever's is the rule, his is the religion*). The result seems chaotic at first sight, but conceals an old story.

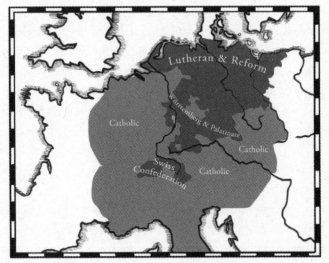

Germany after the Peace of Augsburg, 1555.

The areas of Germany which remained true to Rome had all been part of the Frankish kingdom in 768 AD. Not all that kingdom stayed Catholic—though even in the notionally Calvinist Württemberg and the Palatinate, the population mostly did—but the broad picture would not have surprised Charlemagne or, for that matter, Marcus Aurelius: a revolt against Rome, from the north and the east. The great European fault line wasn't going anywhere. But Europe's place in the world, and hence Germany's place, was.

Germany, Decentered

After Copernicus—that Prussian-born friar-turned-astronomer—Earth was no longer the center of the universe; after Columbus, Europe was no longer the center of the world. The future was on the seven seas.

Germany, with no place on the new oceanic trade routes, was suddenly a political sideshow compared to the world's first transcontinental imperial-ideological struggle, now raging between the Habsburgs and Elizabeth I of England. Meanwhile, the forces of Protestantism and Catholicism in Germany were so finely balanced that, for a half a century after 1555, neither side broke the peace.

It was the Habsburgs who weakened, after the catastrophe of the Armada in 1588. Despite all the wealth of Peru and Mexico, Philip II of Spain had to default on his debts in 1595. Tensions rose as both Catholic and Protestant Germans sensed that change could be in the air.

Things came to a head in 1618 when the new King of Bohemia and Emperor apparent, Ferdinand, an ardent Catholic, tried to rescind a deal he'd done with the Bohemian Protestants. In one of the more memorable scenes in European history, his top officials were thrown from a window—defenestrated—in Prague, and the *Thirty Years War* (1618–48) began.

Apocalypse

The Thirty Years' War was originally yet another round in the ancient struggle over whether any Rome-centered power would ever truly rule over all Germany. This time, the fight was expressed in the new terms of Catholic versus Protestant—at first.

By 1630, the imperial forces, led by the Dutch-Bohemian double act of Generals Tilly and Wallenstein, seemed close to winning. But now Protestant Sweden and Catholic France began to fear total imperial control of Germany. The Catholic regime in Paris subsidized the Lutheran Swedes to intervene against the Catholic Empire. Gustavus Adolphus, the first general to employ highly trained infantry firepower, won an annihilating victory at Breitenfeld in 1631 and instructed his army to *turn Bavaria entirely to waste and ashes*. When he was killed at the Battle of Lützen the following year, the French entered the conflict themselves.

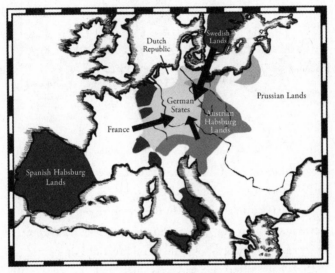

Europe's killing field 1618–48.

It was now in reality a fight between Spanish Habsburgs and French Bourbons, with the disunited little German realms mere pawns or battlefields for the mightier, centralized nations. An entire generation simply gave up trading and even farming, knowing that at any moment another vast and starving army might pass through, leaving nothing but plague and corpses in its wake.

The state of Germany at the *Peace of Westphalia* in 1648 is difficult to describe except in biblical terms. Syria today might give us some idea. At least a third of the entire population seems to have perished, more in some areas. In 1631,

A plate from *Les Grandes Misères de la Guerre* by Jacques Callot (1633).

Magdeburg on the Elbe, Otto the Great's most-favored city, had over 20,000 inhabitants; by 1649, it was 450, the rest having been mostly slaughtered in the streets. Even today, when German children sing their version of *Ladybird, Ladybird, Fly Away Home*, it's not a house that's on fire, but Pomerania.

The chaos after the war was such that nobody really knows exactly how many tiny statelets had come into being: as many as 1,800, according to some estimates. Then there were the 50-odd Free Cities, not forgetting the 60-odd ecclesiastical principalities. No map is remotely comprehensible.

What was to become of this hopelessly failed nation? The answer—for better or worse—lay in the east.

The Flight to the East

After the Thirty Years' War, Europe had a new would-be hegemon. If the relative national populations of Europe were the same now as in 1660, there'd be well over 200 million French. That vast nation was now united and was ruled for an extraordinary

72 years (1643–1715) by the Sun King, Louis XIV. Anything near France stood in her mighty shadow, and the innumerable statelets of western and southern Germany were very near indeed.

Three big German dynasties were luckier. These were the Austrian-branch Habsburgs, the Wettins of Saxony and the newcomers, the Hohenzollerns, who had only been Margraves of Brandenburg since 1415. They all had the priceless advantage of physical distance and buffer states between their core possessions and the French behemoth across the Rhine. Geography equaled fate, again.

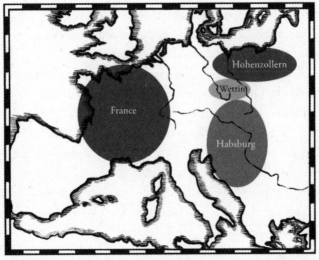

Germany's lucky dynasties.

Friedrich Wilhelm, the new Hohenzollern ruler of Brandenburg-Prussia (the two had joined in 1618) was notionally still a mere duke under the Polish crown; the Poles, Swedes, and Russians all regarded Prussia as a minor, if useful, potential ally in their own wars against one another. By cleverly playing them off, Friedrich Wilhelm managed to get himself declared a fully sovereign duke in 1657, and quietly to build up a professional army. When the hitherto invincible Swedes turned on him, he astonished all Europe on June 18, 1675 by defeating them at the small but spectacular *Battle of Fehrbellin* near Berlin. The *Great Elector*, as he became known, was now a real power: as Duke of Prussia, he was an independent ruler outside the Holy Roman Empire (albeit notionally a Polish vassal); as Margrave of Brandenburg, he was a prestigious Elector within it.

At the same time, the Austrian Habsburgs were reaching new heights of military glory. First, they put together the coalition that drove the Turks from the gates of Vienna in 1683; then, in 1697, Prince Eugene of Savoy shattered the Ottoman army at Zenta, winning at a stroke the entire Kingdom of Hungary, which was far larger than the present-day country.

The Wettin ruler of Saxony, Augustus the Strong, a man who could bend horseshoes with his bare hands and is said to have fathered over 300 children, also turned his attentions to the east. He made himself King of Poland in 1697 by converting to Catholicism, bribing the Polish aristocracy, and winning support from Peter the Great of Russia.

While the eastern Electors flourished, the divided west tried to pull together. The two branches of the Wittelsbach family controlled Bavaria and the Rhineland Palatinate. They now joined with the Electors of Trier, Mainz, and Cologne to form an alliance with France, not just to preserve the peace and law in Germany, but for Christendom (*pour la Chrétienté*). This new, Catholic body was known as the *First Rhine League*. Southern and western Germany were pulling together, free from any eastern connection.

The trouble was, with France so mighty, the League soon became just an instrument of French policy. This dilemma was a rerun of things under the Romans or Charlemagne (and a foreshadow of things under the US occupation post-1945): could Germany ever be truly of the West, yet still remain truly German?

But if the Rhineland seemed too far under French sway, Saxony, Brandenburg-Prussia, and Austria were surely too much of the east? All had their power bases beyond the Elbe or the Danube. How could any of them claim to be the heirs of Charlemagne? Where, then, was the real Germany?

The question only grew more urgent as the sun of France rose higher still.

The French Century

The 18th century in Europe belonged to France. All over Germany, ruinously expensive imitations of Versailles shot up, within whose gilded chambers the German ruling houses, each with its own fawning band of courtiers, took to speaking French. By the mid-18th century, this fashion had trickled down so far that German was on the way to becoming like English after 1066: a Germanic language with an entire Romance vocabulary built onto it from the top down. Here are just a few of the most obvious loanwords: *Champignon, Kostüm, Parfüm, Polizei, Toilette, Omlett, Serviette, Etikette, Charme, Salon, Eleganz, Kompliment, Promenade, Sofa, Balkon, Onkel, Tante, Armee.*

Frederick the Great (1712–86), now full King of Prussia, wrote that German was a half-barbarian tongue in which not even a literary genius could do decent work. Accordingly, he made French the official language of the Prussian Academy of the Arts. Even his own new pleasure palace just outside Berlin got a French name: *Sans Souci.*

The Frenchification of
Germany: Sans Souci.

Patriotic Germans cast about desperately for an alternative. A new generation of writers adored Shakespeare, loved Nature, despised French-style rationalism and declared that emotions were the only way really to know anything. *Feelings are all that matters!* wrote the greatest of them, Johann Wolfgang Goethe (1749–1832).

The Presiding Genius

Goethe is Germany's Shakespeare, Dickens, and Keats, rolled into one. In 1773, when he was 24, his rambunctious Shakespearean tragedy, *Götz von Berlichingen,* blew away French rules on stagecraft. A year later, he smashed "Enlightened" literary taste with his pan-European bestselling tale of youthful romantic suicide, *The Sorrows of Young Werther;* it was the young Napoleon's favorite book and in *Frankenstein,* the monster learns about humanity by reading it. The "Romantic" cult of individual feeling also powers Goethe's early lyric poetry, matchless in the beauty of its pantheistic longing for nature and love; his ballads are among the very few by any self-conscious poet that really feel like strange old folk songs. Later, he more or less invented both the modern novella and the coming-of-age novel. Above everything towers his life's work, the colossal play *Faust,* the tale of the middle-aged intellectual who sells his soul to the devil in return for youth, sex, and power. In the early 20th century, the young Franz Kafka wrote that German writers were still crippled by Goethe's sheer greatness; to this day, educated Germans pepper their conversation thickly with his words.

German culture was back, and it was about to change the rules forever. *Universalism*—the idea that the same cultural norms apply to everyone, everywhere—was denounced as nothing but a cover for French dominion. Instead, every people was said to have its own, unique cultural pathway. The idea took hold among some that, since the elites of Germany had become Frenchified, the only place true Germanness lived on was in the as-yet-unspoiled *Volk* (ordinary people) and their ancient tales. The Brothers Grimm are just the most famous of those who proclaimed that authenticity was to be found in the deep past of land and language, myth and story. This notion is so widely accepted today that many forget its origin as a last resort for a German culture seemingly doomed by French power.

This frantic search for a truly German identity helps to explain why Prussia now became the focus of many patriots.

The Junker State

It seemed an unlikely outcome. Prussia in 1750 had not only a court as Frenchified as any other—more so, even—but also a nasty reputation as a militaristic robber state.

From his father, a terrifying brute, Frederick the Great had inherited an efficient bureaucracy and an army so disproportionately large that Voltaire, who was briefly the favorite at Frederick's court, famously said: *other states have armies; in Prussia, the army has a state.* Frederick's other inheritance was the trauma of having been physically forced to watch his best friend and alleged lover being decapitated. This combination left a man with distinctly psychopathic tendencies (his own nephew, Frederick William, would call him *a real scourge of God, spat into Earth out of Hell by God's wrath*) in command of the most effective army in Europe.

The root of Prussia's military might lay in the deal Frederick's father had made with the Junkers. They were by now far poorer than most western European aristocracies because, while their titles went to all their offspring and their offspring's male offspring, the family's land, often of very poor quality, was held in trust by one son alone. Laws prevented Junkers' estates being sold to non-Junkers, but this also meant they couldn't be mortgaged to make improvements. The net result was an enormous number of proud young men, bred to arms and semicolonial rule, with absolutely no money. But they all had the precious title *von* to their names—something money just couldn't buy. Despite vast differences in wealth and status between them, the Prussian *vons* still recognized each other as a single caste, and many would literally die rather than lose membership of it.

These young men made wonderful officers. They would walk into cannon fire, and drive their men into it too, for the Prussian monarchy, provided their caste was treated as a privileged one by everyone, including the king. Frederick kept his side of the deal: though he abolished serfdom in state lands, he allowed it to continue on Junker estates, and throughout his reign he personally ensured that only noblemen of proper lineage became officers in his army. It was this bargain between Crown and Junkers that made Frederick's Prussia unique.

The moment he took the throne in 1740, Fredrick used his oversized army to rob the Austrians of the province of Silesia, starting a 125-year battle for Germany between the Austrians and the Prussians, two essentially East European powers. That battle was fought out almost entirely on or around the Elbe, from Mollwitz in 1741 to Königgratz in 1866.

Austria almost won when it managed to put together a grand coalition with France and Russia against Prussia in the *Seven Years' War* (1756–63). When that war began, most Germans thought of Prussia as the ancient Greeks thought of Sparta: a grim land filled with ferocious soldiery. But just as Sparta became the savior of Greece at Thermopylae, Prussia now gained huge prestige and even adoration within Germany by whipping a larger French army at Rossbach in 1757.

In their cultural desperation, many Germans couldn't resist the sight of a German power, however unattractive, which could actually stand up to the hegemon of Europe. The cult of Fredrick the Great spread well beyond Prussia, even though he himself had no time at all for it and continued to favor all things French.

The myth of Prussian military invincibility dates from the Seven Years' War. Later Prussian-German historians and generals claimed that Prussia had beaten all comers thanks to its soldiers and Junker officers alike being uniquely disciplined and willing to die for a king who showed sheer, undaunted willpower. In fact, Frederick was beaten several times by the Russians and/or Austrians; after total defeat at Kunersdorf

The Junker Cult of Death for Prussia: Frederick the Great (2nd from r.) mourns the death of a young favorite at Zorndorf (1758).

(1759), he himself wrote from the battlefield to Berlin (in French, naturally) to say that all was lost: *I will not survive the doom of the fatherland. Adieu forever!*

Prussia only survived because Britain, engaged in global war with France, pumped enormous subsidies to Berlin, and because Elizabeth of Russia (who loathed Frederick) died and was succeeded by Peter III (who adored him). Frederick himself called this the *Miracle of the House of Brandenburg*, but later glorifiers of the Prussian army conveniently forgot just how miraculous the escape had been, and how little it had to do with military invincibility.

Frederick soon found common ground with his former enemies, Russia and Austria, in the cynical partitions of Poland (1772–95). For the next century and more, the denial of Poland's existence was to be the one activity which kept Prussia and Russia from each other's throats.

As the 18th century neared its end, western Germany was sandwiched between mighty France across the Rhine and two absolutist powers in the East, Austria and Prussia, both anchored outside any historical definition of Germany, both ruling over numerous non-German peoples, and both now having immense land borders directly with Russia.

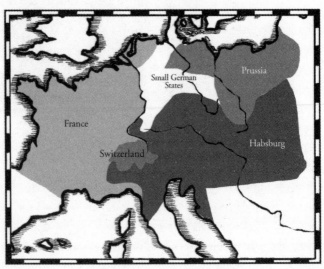

The squeezed West: Germany in 1800.

The only counterweight would be if the west of Germany organized itself at last, and some people began trying. Chief among them was Karl von Dalberg (1744–1817), the Archbishop-Elector of the ancient Roman city of Mainz. He championed the so-called *Third Germany* (or *Trias*) idea that the smaller German states could unite, creating an alternative to both Prussia and Austria.

For a time, Dalberg did indeed become *Prince-Primate* of all western Germany—but in such a way that the whole idea ultimately became discredited. For, just as Caesar had invented Germania in 58 BC, the Third Germany was called into being by the man whom many saw as the new Caesar: Napoleon Bonaparte.

France's Last Fling

During the wars that followed the French Revolution of 1789, most of Europe tried and failed to destroy the new, monarch-free, republican France.

Prussia was the first of the monarchies of Europe to break ranks and do a deal with revolutionary France, after its allegedly invincible army of Junker soldiers had proved distinctly fragile at Valmy (1792). In the *Treaty of Basel* (1795) it secretly recognized France as sole power west of the Rhine (Prussia had had a tiny dynastic toehold there, in Cleves, since 1615), in return for French promises of compensation on the east bank.

Making peace like this, unilaterally, meant an open break with the Austrian-led Holy Roman Empire. Prussia was making a bid to be independently paramount in a neutral North Germany. This explains why, in 1804, a deputation of Rhineland Catholic princes welcomed First Consul Bonaparte during his Charlemagne-themed visit to Aachen, declaring that he was *the first of our Caesars to have crossed the Rhine to drive out the barbarians.* It was a broad hint that the Rhineland Catholics would see the French as liberators, not as conquerors.

Soon, Napoleon made the *Third Germany* a reality. The hero of the revolution having meanwhile become Emperor, he crushed the Russians and Austrians at Austerlitz in 1805, which made him all-powerful in Europe. Prussia had allowed him to march through its territory, and now, as he moved to dissolve the Holy Roman Empire, it hoped to gain from him the official overlordship of North Germany. Napoleon did indeed force the Austrian Emperor Frances II to abdicate, ending the Holy Roman Empire forever. In its place, though, much to the chagrin of the Prussians, he declared that Bavaria, Württemberg, and Saxony were now free kingdoms, the equals of Prussia herself. To add insult to Prussian injury, he called into being the *Confederation of the Rhine.*

Napoleon foils Prussia: The Confederation of the Rhine, 1806.

> Napoleon had read widely in the classics and in history; if he had a hero, a man whose concept of Empire underlay his every move, it was Charlemagne, and the zenith of his power involved the imposition on Europe of his new continental empire with the medieval kingdom of Lotharingia at its core.
>
> Alan Forrest, "Napoleon's Conquest and Its Legacy"

Many people in Germany welcomed French overlordship and the Napoleonic reforms that accompanied it, such as the end of old aristocratic privileges and equality before the law, even for the Jews. Goethe himself was among them: he proudly wore the *légion d'honneur* personally given him by the man he publicly called *my Emperor*.

But a united Western Germany meant the end of Prussia's plans for hegemony in the north. War fever swept Berlin. Fire-breathing Junker officers sharpened their sabers on the steps of the French embassy. Friedrich Wilhelm put his trust in the myth of the Prussian army, the promise of Russian help, and the lateness of the season, which everyone assumed would make a French attack impossible that year. On September 26, 1806, he issued an ultimatum to Napoleon: dissolve the Confederation of the Rhine.

The result should have saved Germany from Prussia forever. Napoleon struck before the Russians could get ready or the autumn rains set in. On October 14, 1806, despite putting over 100,000 men into the field against Napoleon's 80,000, the Prussian Army was routed at the twin *Battles of Jena-Auerstadt.*

> **Queen Louise of Prussia to Her Children After Jena**
> In one day, fate has destroyed the edifice which great men worked to erect over the course of two centuries. There is no Prussian state left, no Prussian army, no national honor left.

Unlike Austria, which was repeatedly defeated by Napoleon yet always bounced back, Prussia simply collapsed. It seemed that Voltaire was right: without the army, Prussia was nothing. Napoleon rode unopposed into Berlin. Prussia still hoped for salvation from the Russians, but when they too were smashed at Friedland, near modern-day Kaliningrad (formerly Prussian Königsberg) in June 1807, the game was up. Napoleon and Tsar Alexander met on a specially built barge floating midstream on the River Memel, the ancient border between East Prussia and Lithuania, leaving King Friedrich Wilhelm on the riverbank, in the pouring rain, awaiting his fate.

Napoleon considered abolishing the Prussian crown altogether. But he was anxious for peace with the Tsar and even hoping to marry their dynasties, so he couldn't show too obvious a contempt for established royalty. He eventually agreed that Prussia might survive, but only as an East Elbian satrap of Russia.

In the *Treaty of Tilsit* (1807) Prussia lost everything west of the Elbe. It was back to where it had started in 1525—just a minor power, beyond what both Caesar Augustus and Charlemagne had considered the natural border of Western Europe. Even east of the Elbe, it was reduced, having been made to cede territory to its hated neighbor and rival, Saxony. Worst of all, it was forced to give up much of its Polish territory and see the Poles re-created as a separate people in the Grand Duchy of Warsaw.

By 1808 the Confederation of the Rhine was misnamed, for it stretched even beyond the Elbe, comprising all that Augustus had called *Germania*.

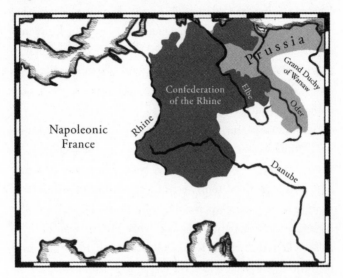

Prussia at bay: The Confederation of the Rhine and the Grand Duchy of Warsaw, 1812.

In the end, it wasn't its own heroism which saved Prussia—and hence doomed Germany—but a fatal miscalculation by Austria.

Soon, the essentially military nature of Napoleon's regime, with its endless demands for taxes and conscripts, and its banning of the Rhineland's lucrative trade with Britain, destroyed west Germany's enthusiasm for French supremacy. But, divided as ever, it had no chance of throwing off the yoke. Prussia, too, stayed meekly onside: it remained loyal to Napoleon during the Anglo-Austrian war against France in 1809; it obediently let him use Prussian territory as the safe base for his invasion of Russia in 1812; it turned down Austrian proposals for an anti-French alliance with Russia in October 1812. Even when Napoleon's catastrophic retreat from Moscow had destroyed the *grande armée*, and the Russians were on the border of East Prussia, the king stayed carefully loyal to Napoleon, offering to court-martial the Prussian General Yorck, who had unilaterally declared his corps to be neutral on December 30, 1812. In short, Prussia didn't rebel openly against Napoleon until he was clearly beaten and the Russians were right at hand. Hardly the stuff of heroic legend.

But now came the great Habsburg failure. Like many Emperors before him, Francis II of Austria had his eye fatally on his non-German interests. Suddenly, he and his great minister, Metternich, decided they were more scared of Russia than of France. In one of the worst calls in history, the Habsburgs, who had for so long fought Napoleon while the Prussian Hohenzollerns kept their heads down, hesitated to join in the attack on the tottering Bonaparte, lest the real winners should be the Russians. Though Austria eventually joined the fight in time to take part in the titanic *Battle of Leipzig* (1813), where each side lost more men than the British Army on the first day of the Somme in 1916, the Habsburgs had missed the patriotic bus. Germany was now freed from French dominion, but Austria seemed to have played little part in the liberation.

With the idea of a *Third Germany* discredited as merely a vehicle for French domination, and with Austria having miscalculated so badly, Prussia was now able, against all reality, to present itself as the natural leader of Germany.

Prussia, Engorged

After Napoleon's first defeat in 1814, Britain and Russia fell out even more swiftly than America and Russia after 1945. The great beneficiary, in this case, was Prussia.

At the *Congress of Vienna* in 1814 the Prussians demanded all Saxony as their reward for having risen up (however belatedly) against Napoleon. The Russians, seeing them as mere clients, backed their claims. The Austrians resisted, and the British agreed with them. Scarcely six months after Napoleon's abdication and exile to Elba, Britain entered into an alliance with France and Austria to resist Russia and Prussia, by war if need be. Russia backed down, so Prussia had no choice but to follow suit, furious, and accept the consolation prize the British were offering: half of Saxony plus a great chunk of the Rhineland.

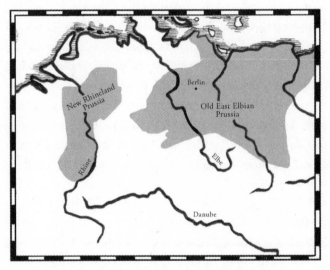

Britain's great folly: Prussia gets the Rhineland (1814).

London had a master plan. Some decent-sized German power should be given major territory straddling the Rhine, to make it a natural guard against any future French expansion. No one—Bavaria, Austria, or Prussia—wanted the job, since it would put them right in the line of fire. Nor did the Prussians much like the idea of having to assimilate new territory which was thoroughly Catholic, with entirely non-Prussian social and legal traditions. For now, though, it was the only thing on offer, so they took it.

The Rhinelanders were not consulted. But what Prussia at first saw as a consolation prize was perhaps the most advanced commercial and industrial area of the world outside Britain itself.

Then, in 1815, Prussia got even luckier. Napoleon returned from exile, and with Russia, Austria, Prussia, and Britain united against him, his only chance was to beat one or two of them right away. By seeking battle in the north, he chose to meet the British and the Prussians first. The glory of ending Napoleon forever at Waterloo thus fell to Britain's Duke of Wellington and the Prussian General Blücher. Later British and German historians would argue bitterly about who had truly won the battle, but at the time, no one cared. Prussia was now the darling of the mighty British. They laughed with delight when Blücher came to London to be feted as Britain's co-victor, got his first look at the fantastic wealth on display there, and cried: *What a splendid city to plunder!*

Germany After Waterloo: A Land in Winter

After Waterloo, the victorious powers at the Congress of Vienna all wanted to turn the clock back to before the French Revolution. In France, this clearly meant restoring the monarchy, but the Holy Roman Empire had died, unlamented, in 1806. In its place was set up a simplified and modernized version, the *German Confederation*, with Austria as its permanent president.

It wasn't really German and it wasn't really a confederation either, if by that we mean a union of equals. The 38 member-states included the Kings of Denmark and Holland (as hereditary dukes of Holstein and Luxembourg, respectively) and the two dominant powers, Prussia and Austria, both also ruled large territories outside it.

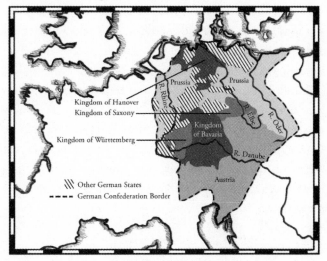

The German Confederation after Waterloo (1815).

For the next fifty years, German politics were determined by the rivalry between Prussia and Austria, and by the inability of the smaller states to find enough common ground to give up their ancient *particularism* (as it was called) and forge an effective union.

The one thing which united the Austrian and Prussian crowns, and united them both with the other kings and princes of Europe, was a hatred of German nationalism. In this age, nationalism was seen as progressive and politically liberal, because it demanded that a people (ethnically defined) should rule themselves, not be ruled by whoever happened to have inherited their thrones. Naturally, hereditary rulers all over Europe loathed and feared nationalism.

At first, the rivalry between Prussia and Austria was disguised by this shared interest. With their mighty neighbor, Russia, they created the *Holy Alliance* (September 26, 1815), to keep Europe safe for autocracy. They then led the smaller states of the German Confederation into the grand clampdown of the *Carlsbad Decrees* (1819), which declared that any display of liberal/nationalist sentiment, even by a sporting club or university lecturer, was seditious, demagogical, and illegal.

A stultifying social, political, and bureaucratic conformism now descended on all Germany, most memorably described in Heinrich Heine's (1797–1856) great poem-cycle *Germany: A Winter's Tale*. Here, the poet, who has fled Germany, returns full of romantic thoughts—only to find himself confronted by the Prussian soldiers who now run the Rhineland:

> *Still the same old wooden pedants*
> *A nation that can still only move*
> *At right angles, faces frozen*
> *In that old arrogance . . .*

In this Germany, social mobility was nonexistent, high government or army service was reserved for aristocrats, and active politics was forbidden. The one place you could still make a glittering career was by going to university and dedicating yourself to studying languages, history, theology, music, science—anything with no obvious political application. The middle-class cults of *inwardness (Innerlichkeit)* and *cultural education (Bildung)* grew up; German universities, being the sole outlet for social ambition, rapidly became the wonders of the world. With real political discussion banned, German university philosophers became masters at teasing out abstract notions of freedom, duty, belonging, and suchlike. By far the most influential of these thinkers was G. W. F. Hegel (1770–1831), who is still very widely studied.

Hegel

Hegel veiled his thinking in such *senseless, meaningless webs of language* (Schopenhauer) that it's often almost impossible to work out what he really means. But at its heart is his *dialectical* theory of history. This states that ideas are always in open or secret conflict; these conflicts create change, not by slow evolution but in sudden great upheavals whose results are impossible to predict (e.g., the rise of Napoleon out of the French Revolution). This was radical stuff indeed, and his listeners thrilled to it. However, Hegel didn't think it was a random process: he believed that the *World Spirit* (*der Weltgeist*) was always leading things in the general direction of the perfect *Rational State*. This did not yet exist, he said, but he often suggested that Prussia—in truth the most repressive and militarized state in Western Europe—was the nearest thing yet to it. Hegel's influence on German 19th-century thought, and on some thinkers to this day, is incalculably baneful.

Hegel: the root of all evil?

If you wanted to say or write, let alone do, anything critical of the state of affairs in poor, oppressed Germany, you had one simple option: get out. Britain, the *workshop of the world*, had a limitless demand for labor, absolutely uncontrolled borders, no limits or even registrations of residence, and a policy of never handing over anyone to any foreign power for any reason whatever. London became the most-favored destination of German exiles, whether they were seekers of political asylum or simple economic migrants.

From *The Penny Satirist*, March 1840.

From there you could always go on to the even greater freedom of America, as many did. The dream of Anglo-American liberty became the natural vision for liberal Germans desperate for an alternative to the Russian-backed Prussian and Austrian police states.

England's Natural Ally

Instead of fleeing to England, some Germans sought out a special relationship with her.

> ### Nineteenth-Century Anglo-Saxon Liberalism
> Britain's prestige and power were at an all-time high. Political liberals everywhere accepted that the path of constitutional rule, light-handed government, free trade, ever-increasing wealth and almost unlimited personal liberty was not just the supposed story of Britain (and America) but was in fact the natural way of the world itself. All countries would eventually follow this Anglo-Saxon path, perhaps with a dose of swift military persuasion where truly necessary. The last living high priests of this ideology are American neoconservatives like Dick Cheney, architect of the Gulf Wars.

The brand-new field of linguistic scholarship had revealed that there were distinct groups of languages in Europe. Since English clearly belonged to the *Germanic* group, it was claimed that some timeless affinity existed between the Germans and the English. In the first three-quarters of the 19th century, it was common for the English and the Germans to write about each other as *cousins*. This led some Germans to believe that Anglo-Saxon liberty was in fact an ancient *Germanic* idea, not some foreign, western imposition like those the French (and indeed the Romans) had tried to bolt onto Germany.

Hegel himself mused on the possibility that *World History* would next be revealed in *the Nordic principle of the Germanic peoples* as a sea-going, colonial *Empire of the Germans* (*Reich der Germanen*), by which he meant a post-Waterloo alliance of Protestant Germany—led, naturally, by Prussia—and England.

This wasn't just a philosopher's dream. It obsessed one of the most politically influential Germans on the planet. Albert of Saxe-Coburg, Prince Consort of Britain's Queen Victoria (herself, of course, of German family) was tireless in pursuit of what was called the *Coburg Plan*. Backed by King Leopold of Belgium among others, Albert and his German advisers proposed that Prussia should first reform along British constitutional lines, then unite all of Germany, which in the process would become (as Victoria put it*) a most useful ally* for Britain.

Prince Albert's *Coburg Plan.*

The Failed Revolution of 1848–49

The time seemed ripe in 1848. Harvests had failed everywhere and all Europe was swept by a wave of revolutions. In Germany, the immediate inspiration was the revolution in France, but when the demonstrators came together in Mannheim on the Rhine to frame their actual demands, these were based on Anglo-American manifestos for change (rather more American than Anglo):

> **The German Revolution Demands:**
> 1) Armed militias with freely elected officers.
> 2) Unconditional freedom of the press.
> 3) Jury courts on the English model.
> 4) Immediate creation of an all-German parliament.
> 5) A Bill of Rights for citizens.
> 6) An agreed constitution.
>
> *March Demands*, February 27, 1848

On March 18, 1848, 300 demonstrators were killed fighting the army in the streets of Berlin (the *Square of the 18th of March* in front of the Brandenburg Gate is today named after this event). Friedrich Wilhelm IV lost his nerve at the body-count, bowed his head to the fallen revolutionaries, publicly adopted their black-red-gold flag, and made the public promise that *from this moment, Prussia will dissolve into Germany.*

The liberal-nationalist revolutionaries seemed to have won. Prussia itself now had an apparently liberalized king and an elected parliament (the *Landtag*). Meanwhile in Frankfurt, a larger, all-German parliament (the *Reichstag*) met to discuss the shape of German Unification. Would it be a *Greater German* solution (including and led by Austria) or a *Little German* one (excluding Austria, led by Prussia)?

It was to be neither. By the time the Frankfurt Parliament offered the crown of all Germany to Frederick Wilhelm IV of Prussia on April 3, 1849, things had changed and he scornfully turned it down. For Austria and Prussia had a black ace up their sleeves: Russia. They knew they could call on the Tsar's mighty armies of loyal peasants, who'd been unaffected by liberal ideas. The west-facing revolution of 1848–49 was smashed, and the autocracies of Germany restored to full power, thanks to the unimpaired health of Russian despotism.

It was now only a question of whether Prussia or Austria would rule Germany, with Russian approval, naturally. Prussia moved swiftly, trying to dragoon the other big northern German kingdoms, Saxony and Hanover, into the *Erfurt Union*. But Austria was ready for a fight. Both sides mobilized. The all-powerful Tsar Nicholas backed the status quo. Prussia had to stand down at the *Humiliation of Olmütz* (November 29, 1850) and accept the restoration of the German Confederation of 1815, with Austria still as its president.

The West, Rampant

In 1850, things in Germany were back to where they'd been in 1815: Austria and Prussia in standoff, with Russia looming over them both. German exiles, economic and political, continued to flee to London. One political asylum seeker settled to write his books there, with the goal (as he put it), not just of understanding the world but of changing it.

Karl Marx

Marx made his name as a witty, drinking-and-dueling, fearlessly radical reporter and newspaper publisher. In the *Communist Manifesto*, he and his fellow Rhinelander, Friedrich Engels, took Hegel's doctrine of progress-through-conflict and proclaimed that the real battle which powered all history was between the social classes. This *class struggle* would continue until Marx's version of Hegel's *rational state* came about with the *dictatorship of the proletariat*. All conflicts would then cease, true freedom (as opposed to so-called freedom on the Anglo-Saxon model) would be universal, and history would come to an end. In later life, Marx considered himself not a polemicist but a scientist, like Darwin, whom he greatly admired for having (said Marx) provided *a basis in natural science for the historical class struggle*. His vast *Das Kapital* claimed to prove it scientifically inevitable that capitalism would collapse violently. The messianic angle to all this talk of *inevitability, history, true freedom, struggle* and so on is very clear and, as tends to happen with messianic thought, Marx's has been widely used to justify terrible despots and killers. It may be best to think of Marx as a top-class journalist who was often strikingly insightful about the immediate past and the present, but almost always entirely wrong about the future.

Then, however, came a great shift in the balance of European power. In 1853 the term *Western Powers* (*Westmächte*) entered the German language. France and Britain united to oppose Russia's expansion into the Black Sea in the *Crimean War* (1853–56), which they saw as an ideological conflict of liberalism vs absolutism. The Tsar's armies were beaten on his own territory, dealing an epochal blow to Russian power and prestige. Straight afterward, Britain crushed the Indian Mutiny (1857). With the British globally victorious and the Americans not yet mired in the Civil War, the future, in the late 1850s, looked distinctly Anglo-Saxon.

In Germany, anglophilia reached new heights, boosted by the engagement in 1856 of Victoria and Albert's daughter (another Victoria) to Frederick, second in line to the throne of Prussia. A relatively unknown Junker lawyer and politician, Otto von Bismarck, wrote in disgust to a friend:

> **Bismarck Rails Against Anglicization, 1856:**
> This stupid admiration of the average German for Lords
> and Guineas, the anglomania of parliament, of the news-
> papers, of sportsmen, of landlords, and of presiding judges.
> Even now, every Berliner feels himself elevated if a real
> English jockey talks to him and gives him the chance to
> grind out the crushed fragments of the Queen's English.
> How much more so it will be when the First Lady of this
> land is an Englishwoman?
>
> Letter written between May 2–4, 1856

If Berlin itself was anglophile, the feeling was even stronger in
the Prussia-ruled (since 1815) Rhineland. The Cologne-based
National League (*Nationalverein*) saw the future in a new,
ocean-going Anglo-American-German world hegemony that
had nothing to do with the old Prussia-Russia axis.

> The Germanic race is destined by fate to rule the world.
> She is physically and mentally privileged above all other
> races, and half the Earth is virtually subject to her.
> England, America, and Germany: these are the three
> branches of the mighty Germanic tree.
>
> *Wochen-Blatt des Nationalvereins*, September 7, 1865

The Rhineland was looking west. Russian influence was
waning and Prussia, which had been for fifty years little
more than a Russian client, no longer felt so invincible.
Tensions between old Prussia east of the Elbe and its new
Rhineland colony now burst into the open.

At the heart of the conflict was money. The Rhineland
made most of the wealth in Prussia; the Berlin court decided

where taxes were spent. But as industrial boom led to huge population growth, more and more of the MPs in the Prussian Parliament, plus more and more of the money in Berlin's coffers, came from this west-facing region. The power struggle became centered on funds for the Prussian army. Almost the single real lever the Prussian Parliament

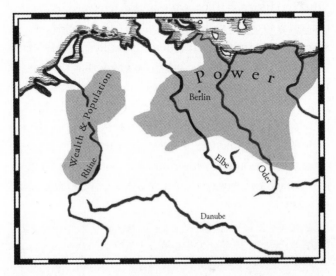

had retained after the crushing of liberalism in 1849 was that it could still approve or refuse the state budget. Rhineland MPs, and liberal MPs from Berlin itself, now insisted that they'd only vote for bigger funds for the army if it became a people's militia, with officers appointed by parliament. This was complete anathema to the king and the Junkers.

By 1862, liberal pressure was so great that Wilhelm I seriously considered abdicating in favor of his son. That would have put Queen Victoria's beloved son-in-law Frederick, who was known to favor reform, on the throne of Prussia. The reactionary clique around Wilhelm saw this as the end of things. They suggested one last throw of the dice: appoint a true East Elbian Junker who would tough it out with the west-facing parliamentarians. And they had a candidate in mind.

Enter the Iron Chancellor

Otto von Bismarck (1815–98) was as determined to preserve old, royal Prussia as any other Junker. On the one hand, his success rested simply on the uniquely ruthless pursuit of this one ambition. But on the other, he knew that the wave of liberal nationalism could only be channeled, not resisted. In June 1862, in London, before he even took over in Prussia, he told Benjamin Disraeli, Britain's future PM, exactly how he intended to go about it. Disraeli, astonished (as people often were) by how openly Bismarck spoke, set it all down in his diary and warned the Austrians: *Take care of that man; he means what he says.*

Bismarck Tells It Straight, June 1862

I shall soon be compelled to undertake the conduct of the Prussian government . . . As soon as the army shall have been brought to such a condition as to inspire respect, I shall seize the first best pretext to declare war against Austria, dissolve the German Confederation, subdue the minor states and give national unity to Germany under Prussian leadership.

Under Prussian leadership were the vital words. Bismarck planned to give Germany what looked like national unity, but was really Prussian dominion. His great bet was that many Germans were by now so desperate for unity that with some clever window dressing, they wouldn't notice, or care, that this was actually a royal Prussian takeover.

He was soon given a chance to convince German nationalists that Prussia, not the West, was their true friend. In late 1863, Denmark seemed about to fully incorporate the twin duchies of Schleswig-Holstein, which were held dynastically by its king, but where most people spoke German. The German Confederation tried to invade, using troops from Hanover and Saxony, but with little success. During the stalemate that followed, Britain noisily promised to back Denmark if it came to renewed fighting.

Patriotic outrage swept Germany. Why did the Englanders, who championed Greek and Italian nationalism, not do the same for their German relations? Bismarck saw his opportunity to call Britain's bluff and at the same time involve the Austrians in a joint action that was bound to provide opportunities for dispute. He offered to send in the Prussian army, ostensibly in the name of the German Confederation. Austria had little option but to follow suit or yield its theoretical leadership of Germany. The Danes were quickly beaten—and the promised Royal Navy never appeared.

Bismarck had correctly gambled that the richest nation on Earth was not ready for a fight. After 1864, many German nationalists lost their old admiration for England, seeing it instead as a decadent, mangy old lion only bothered about its bank account.

Though he had cleverly harnessed national liberal passion, Bismarck had by no means tamed it. The parliamentary conflict in Berlin about funding and/or reforming the Prussian army grew still hotter. In June 1865, in the parliament itself,

Britain's feebleness in 1864, mocked in *Kladderadatsch*.

Bismarck furiously challenged the great liberal leader Dr. Rudolf Virchow, father of cellular biology, to a duel. It's said that Virchow, knowing he had no chance against the giant and ferocious Junker with either sword or pistol, chose as his weapon a pair of *bratwurst*, one of which would be poisoned. The duel never took place, but things couldn't go on like this, and Bismarck knew it. It was time to enact the plan he'd so boldly outlined to Disraeli in 1862.

Prussia Defeats Germany

Bismarck marched troops into Holstein on June 9, 1866. His plan did not rely on the mythical invincibility of the Prussian army. Instead, he had made sure in advance that the diplomatic scales were perfectly weighted. When the fighting started on June 16, Russia and France stayed neutral, while Italy attacked Austria's possessions in Venetia. Crucially, the Habsburgs were faced with a war on two fronts.

Most of Germany, including all the other full kingdoms (Bavaria, Hanover, Saxony, and Württemberg) backed Austria.

But unlike Prussia, they hadn't been planning a war, so they were completely unready for it. Still, they fought. On June 27, the Hanoverians beat the Prussians at Langensalza: if the Prussian Army gave battle hastily and outnumbered, it lost, like any other army. But everything really depended on Austria.

Fatally, and like so many imperial German champions of Rome before them, the Austrian Habsburgs couldn't bring themselves to prioritize their position within Germany above all else. They could have let the Italians have Venice and faced Prussia full-on. Instead, they split their forces almost exactly in two. When the decisive battle was fought, on the banks of the Elbe at Königgratz (now Hradec Králové in the Czech Republic) on July 3, 1866, only half of Austria's strength was there, so the numbers were even.

The weaponry was not. Thanks to the wealth generated by the Rhineland, the Prussians had just upgraded to breech-loading rifles, whereas the Austrians had thought about it, but had balked at the vast expense. Like everyone else in Europe, they still only used muzzle-loaders. The Prussian infantry could fire repeatedly from kneeling or even prone positions, like modern armies; the Austrians still had to stand and reload with ramrods, as armies had done half a century before at Waterloo. It doesn't take military genius to win a numerically even fight when your infantry's kill ratio is 4:1. The Austrians were mown down and routed.

Led by the Bavarians, the southern states fought small battles against the Prussians for another three weeks but with Austria knocked out, there was no hope. The duchies of Schleswig-Holstein, Hesse-Kassel, Frankfurt, and Nassau were annexed by Prussia. In Hanover, which had resisted hardest, the Guelph family, the oldest monarchy in Europe, was deposed. The kingdom was reduced to a province of Prussia and its large gold reserves physically stolen. This was conquest, pure and simple.

All Germany was now at Prussia's mercy. The king wanted to march on Vienna. The army was all for it. But Bismarck had never wanted any more of Germany than could be safely prussianized, and he called a halt. It was time for Prussia to digest her huge gains.

The North German Confederation (*Norddeutscher Bund*) was now founded to provide a constitutional fig leaf for de facto Prussian hegemony. It was notionally a federal state with individual members and free elections, but the King of Prussia was always to be the head of it, and the First Minister of Prussia was always to be the Confederation's Chancellor. Over 80% of the population and territory were Prussian.

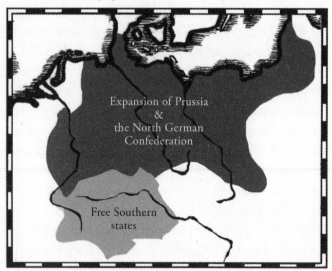

Expansion of Prussia
&
the North German
Confederation

Free Southern
states

The North German Confederation, 1867.

Saxony was forced to join, but the states south of the River Main—Bavaria, Württemberg, Baden, and Hessen-Darmstadt—

were left free. Bismarck now staged elections to an all-German *Customs Parliament* (*Zollparlament*) in Berlin. He expected that popular nationalist feeling would make itself known, forcing the still-free rulers to accept union under Prussia. But he was disappointed: All four southwestern electorates voted decisively for anti-Prussian candidates. To them, the difference between unity and prussianization was clear. This is hardly surprising since they'd fought actual battles against Prussia only two years before.

The die was not yet cast. To complete his grand plan of 1862 (*subdue the minor states*) Bismarck now needed France to attack Prussia. Only this would enable him to pose as the defender of western Germany, rather than its conqueror.

In the crowning debacle of his disastrous later years, the aging and infirm Napoleon III duly obliged. On July 13, 1870, Bismarck's deadly mix of Junker banditry and Modernist understanding gave birth to a brand new beast: war led by mass media. He personally doctored an otherwise unremarkable diplomatic note—the *Ems telegram*—so that it seemed as though Prussia's King William had insulted the French ambassador. He then published it, to give maximum offense to French public opinion, on Bastille Day. Napoleon III saw a chance to recover his fading popularity. Assured by his generals that his army was ready, he declared war.

The world, knowing nothing of Bismarck's plan, fell for it completely and saw only a wanton French attack. Karl Marx declared a week into hostilities that it was a French *war plot*, with Germany (not just Prussia) fighting *a war of defense against Bonapartist aggression*. Most people expected a long fight on German soil, with France's professional army the likely victors over Prussia's conscripts. In London, people sang *The Watch o'er the Rhine*. Austria rubbed her hands at the thought of revenge for 1866 once Prussia was defeated.

No one knew that Bismarck and the Prussian General Staff under Helmuth von Moltke had been planning this very war for several years. Bismarck carefully secured Russian neutrality, so that no forces needed to be left in the east; Moltke used the railway system to get troops to the front more swiftly than anyone thought possible; and in Krupp's new rifled-steel, breach-loading artillery (forged in the industrial lands so fatefully given to Prussia by Britain in 1815), the Prussians possessed a step-change in military technology. Out-planned, outnumbered in every battle and catastrophically outgunned, the French never stood a chance.

To contemporaries, it seemed astounding. A wave of nationalist fever swept Germany as the centuries-old shadow of French hegemony was blasted away. Paris itself was besieged and in their euphoria or megalomania, the Prussian army insisted, against Bismarck's initial resistance, that it was militarily necessary to take Alsace and Lorraine. These had been French for several generations and (judging by their voting habits for the next twenty years) the vast majority of the people would have been content to stay that way, even though they mostly spoke dialects of German. The annexation was to prove an immobile block to Franco-German relations.

The south German kingdoms, whose contingents had found themselves part of this amazing victory, now began to negotiate entrance to the North German Confederation, though with clauses to guard their own autonomy. Suddenly, on December 10, 1870, the North German Confederation declared that it was now an Empire, and that the

King of Prussia was its Emperor. Bismarck made it clear to the southwest that backing out now was not an option.

On the morning of January 18, 1871, in the Hall of Mirrors at Versailles, Bismarck, and Wilhelm I appeared in high ill humor, having been locked all night in a bitter, table-thumping argument about whether Wilhelm would be called *German Emperor* or *Emperor of Germany*. The Grand Duke of Baden solved the problem by simply crying out *long live the Emperor Wilhelm*. In strictly legal terms, the day had no more significance than the day the Berlin Wall fell, but history doesn't work in strictly legal terms. The Second German Empire was now a fact.

The southwest of Germany, which had been a constituent part of Western Europe since 100 AD, was now completely in the hands of a power from beyond the Elbe which had only existed for three and a half centuries. The center of gravity in Europe had shifted dramatically eastward. Disraeli immediately saw this and proclaimed in a speech to the House of Commons that this was *a greater political event than the French revolution of last century.*

The New Paradigm

The new German Empire was founded in a heady atmosphere of victory, and its economy, fed by trainloads of free gold bullion from occupied France, boomed immediately. From the start, it was clearly a strange animal.

It didn't include over eight million people who had, until 1871, always thought of themselves as German—in Austria, Bohemia and Moravia—but it did contain three million Poles, as well as large, recently-conquered Danish and French minorities in Schleswig-Holstein and Alsace-Lorraine, who had no intention of becoming Germans.

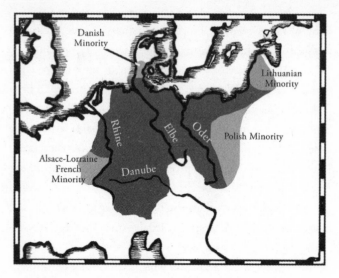

The German Empire of 1871–1914, showing minority groups.

No Germany, even of the imagination, had ever looked like this. For many years, foreign observers regularly called it *Prussia-Germany* or even simply *Prussia*.

This empire seemed perfectly designed to be impossible for anyone but Bismarck to run. As well as the imperial *Reichstag* in Berlin, every state also had its own *Landtag*. But since Prussia was now so vast, the Prussian *Landtag* (also in Berlin) actually ran day-to-day business in two-thirds of the entire Empire. It had a unique three-tiered electoral system where the weight of a citizen's vote depended on how much tax he paid. In rural constituencies of East Elbia, which typically had a couple of big estates, almost no middle class, and many obedient peasants, Junker landowners virtually chose MPs for their very own *Konservative Partei*.

The Reichstag, just down the road, was elected on universal male suffrage. But its MPs could not get rid of the chancellor; only the emperor could do that. So long as Bismarck retained

King Wilhelm's confidence, all MPs could do was refuse his bills or budgets, forcing new elections. If that happened, Bismarck himself frequently hinted, he might unleash his scar-faced Junker samurai and their savagely drilled farm boys.

> When the debate is over and the vote is about to be taken ... a door opens and in strides Prince Bismarck, in cuirassier uniform with huge jackboots and an enormous sword which he clatters along the floor. The House is crushed and acts as though these military statesmen had behind them a regiment of the line ready to enforce obedience at the point of a bayonet.
>
> Henry Vizetelly, *Berlin Under the New Empire*,
> London, 1878

Bismarck was able to keep up democratic appearances because there was a big party in the Reichstag that was in practice loyal to him alone. This party was the *National Liberals*, whose power base was Prussia and the smaller Protestant states. They are central to German political history after 1871.

The National Liberals had split away from the old liberals after the war of 1866 and developed their own, unique spin on Victorian liberal thought. They believed in Progress and Freedom, of course—but in a rather new way. To them, Progress didn't mean delivering more, messy, individualistic, so-called freedom. Mankind's real Freedom (as Hegel had claimed) lay in belonging to a smoothly functioning state—like the new Prussian-German Empire. It wasn't perfect yet, of course, but success in war and business was the Darwinian proof that it was on the right lines. Therefore (so went National Liberal logic) Bismarck should be supported to the hilt.

In this alliance between Bismarck's new Empire and the ideology of Progress-through-Conflict we first see the great pillars of every full-blown modern dictatorship, in embryonic form:

Worship of state as font of "true" freedom **+** Ideology of "inevitable progress through conflict" **+** One-man rule with sham parliament, backed by army **=** Second German Empire—and all modern dictatorships

The God of Progress Fails

Bismarck almost immediately declared war on the social and political influence of the Catholic Church in what was known as the *Cultural Struggle* (*Kulturkampf*). Schools were to be taken out of Church control, civil marriages allowed and priests forbidden from engaging in anything that could be termed political opposition.

Foreign observers were baffled: gratuitously picking a fight with just-annexed southern Germany and the Polish minority in Prussia seemed a strange way to unite the new Empire. But Bismarck didn't want unification. He wanted prussianization—and his vital allies, the National Liberals, wanted Progress. Fighting the Catholic Church was the one sure way to join these political dots.

Soon, however, this strange new imperial project was in a complete shambles. The almighty boom had been built on robbed French gold; as soon as it dried up an almighty crash followed. It took 40 years for the Berlin stock exchange to get back to the high of late 1872. The experience was seared into the German language as the *Age of the Founders* (*Gründerjahre*)—meaning not the founders of the new empire, but founders of dubious, speculative companies. While the economy tanked, the Catholic population and the Church held out against the *Kulturkampf*. State repression grew so harsh that even the Prussian Conservatives refused to back it. In the end, all Bismarck achieved was to succor the Catholics' very own new political vehicle, the Centre Party, which became for over two decades the largest single party in the Reichstag. Meanwhile the German socialists united in 1875 under a Marxian banner and their rival take on Progress—one which ended in the millennium of World Revolution—started to score electoral successes.

Bismarck considered another war to shore up his rule. In 1875 he used his tame press to hint that a new strike on France might be in sight. The *War in Sight Crisis* led to the supposedly impossible: Britain and Russia made moves to ally with France against Prussia-Germany. Bismarck had to beat a hasty retreat, furiously claiming that *the Englishwoman*—the Crown Princess—had betrayed him to Queen Victoria.

Nothing was going right for the new Prussia-Germany. Then it got worse.

Bismarck Dooms Germany

From 1876, a wave of Pan-Slav nationalism swept southeastern Europe, which was still ruled by the Turkish Ottoman Empire. Russia successfully attacked the Turks in 1877 and now posed as the protector of all Slavs everywhere. This was potentially fatal to the Austro-Hungarian Habsburg Empire. It had come perilously close to collapse after its defeat by Prussia in 1866. Now, if its Poles, Slovenes, Serbs, Croats, and Czechs rose up, backed by Russia, it would be finished. The ruling German minority would surely want to flee into the new German Empire, and all Germany would surely demand they be let in.

To Bismarck, this would be disaster. He had never wanted a united Germany, just a Prussian Germany. If eight million more Catholic Germans were received into the Empire—if Vienna joined Munich and Stuttgart as counterweights to Berlin, and with a Habsburg king on board to boot—Prussia's game would be up.

For Prussia to keep ruling over Germany, the multinational Austro-Hungarian Empire had to be kept afloat at all costs. As Bismarck admitted to Disraeli on June 17, 1878, he was *bound hand and foot to Austria*.

So Bismarck made a U-turn that astonished the world: he called off the *Kulturkampf,* broke with the liberals, abandoned Free Trade and, in October 1879, signed an anti-Russian defensive alliance with his oldest enemy, arch-Catholic Austria.

The *Dual Alliance* of 1879 was a terrible deal for Germany. There was nothing in the diplomatic air that might make Russia attack Germany, whereas the frictions between Russia and Austria-Hungary in the Balkans were very real. Now, if the Habsburgs could just goad Russia into drawing first, they'd have the whole might of a united Germany to back them in their adventures beyond the Danube.

In 1815 and 1850, Vienna had wanted to have its cake and eat it, by remaining a vast, only part-German dynastic empire, yet also determining all-German policy. In 1879, it got exactly that. For the side that had been whipped by Prussia in 1866, it was an amazing comeback. No sane German statesman would ever have agreed to it.

Bismarck wasn't insane. But he wasn't really *German*, either. He was Prussian. And to safeguard Prussian rule over Germany, he forged the military union with Austria in the full knowledge that *some damn stupid thing in the Balkans*—the words are his own—could condemn all Germany to war with Russia.

The old, west-facing kingdoms and duchies of Germany now faced being dragged by Prussia into a Balkan conflict between the eastern Germans and the Slavs that had nothing to do with them.

Darkness Visible

Bismarck's change of course in 1879 was so drastic that historians talk about *the second foundation of the Empire*. It left one particular group in Germany floundering: people who self-defined as *Protestant* Germans. They were mostly in the north and east, but had local power bases elsewhere, in lands whose rulers had backed Luther, or in towns developed later as Prussian administrative bastions. The state-sponsored *Kulturkampf* against the Catholics had radicalized them—but in 1879 they found themselves dumped by Bismarck in favor of deals with Catholics and conservatives. These embittered acolytes of Progress now made being Protestant German into a new ersatz religion of alien-free *German-ness (Deutschtum)*. Anti-Catholicism was second nature to them, but the fatal spine of the movement was a brand new kind of anti-Semitism.

The great proclaimer of this was the official Prussian State Historian, Heinrich von Treitschke, guru of the National Liberals, whose prestige was vast and whose *drum-like shriek,* as one American observer called it, frequently enthralled the

Reichstag. Treitschke's 1879 article *Our Prospects* (*Unsere Aussichten*), better known as its shorter 1880 form *A Word about Our Jews,* is the founding document of modern political anti-Semitism. From now on, hating the Jews wasn't just about hating the Jews; it was a fully fledged ideology, unlike any other form of racism.

To Treitschke, the Jews were *our misfortune.* They had a deep, mysterious relationship with the *Englanders* (about whom he had long raged). Like the English, they were personally degenerate and cowardly, with the mentality of shopkeepers rather than heroes, yet somehow—in contradiction of all true Progress!—they ran the world. Ruthless, globalizing, culture-less, finance-driven Modernity was the Anglo-Jewish master plan. More healthy but simpler nations, like the Germans, were putty in their hands. Every anti-Semite since Treitschke has signed up to this conspiracy theory: Kaiser Wilhelm II talked of *Judaengland* just as modern anti-Semites do of *Jew York.*

Treitchske added an extra Prussian spin for his readers. *From the inexhaustible womb of Poland,* he claimed, came *an annual swarm of ambitious young Jewish trouser-peddlers whose children and grandchildren will rule the press and stock exchanges of Germany.* He thus neatly managed to link fear of allegedly Jewish/ Anglo-Saxon modernity with the ancient Prussian colonial fear and loathing of Poland. The Jews were painted as internationalist, money-bagged internal Englanders and penniless, fast-breeding Polish immigrants, rolled into one.

To radical Protestants, the Jews henceforth joined in dark union with the Catholic Church as foreign bodies within Prussian German-ness. The cry went up: *Without the Jews, without Rome, we shall build the cathedral of Germania* (*Ohne Juda, ohne Rom, bauen wir Germanias Dom*).

Nor would there be anywhere for the old Junker aristocracy in this new, Germanic cathedral. The rabid young librarian Dr. Otto Böckel won his Reichstag seat from the Junkers's own Conservative Party in 1887 with the catchy slogan *Jews, Junkers and Priests all belong in the same pot (Jude, Junker und Pfaffen gehören in einen Topf).* His allies compiled a notorious handbook called the *Semi-Gotha*, which listed all the nobility allegedly tainted by Jewish blood.

For this new anti-Semitism was a socially radical movement. It claimed that what true German-ness needed was a new aristocracy of race, not of family. Leaders of the *Anti-Semitic People's Party,* the *German Social Anti-semitic Party,* the *Pan-German League,* the *German Reform Party* and suchlike often gave themselves forged titles and by 1908, one false aristocrat, Lanz "von" Liebenfels, was already flying the swastika flag at his castle. *National Protestantism* (as historians often call it) sometimes slid into pure Germanic paganism.

The National Protestant Vision, 1902

The belief of the Germanic tribes is the Christianity of the Reformation. Protestant Christianity is a belief which does not crush German nature, that nature so full of power and resistance, but rather unfolds it... Protestantism is the rock on which the culture of the German tribes, of the Germanic race, is built. Protestantism is the fundament of its political power, of its moral virtues, of its dauntless, victorious science.

C. Werkshagen, *Der Protestantismus am Ende des XIX Jahrhundert in Wort und Bild,* Berlin 1902.

In 1893, candidates who made anti-Semitism their main platform (half of them actually called themselves *Anti-semites* on the ballot slips) won sixteen Reichstag seats, all of them in rural, Protestant Prussia, Saxony, and Hesse. What followed is a lesson to any country with a noisy, radical minority.

Those sixteen seats on their own meant little. But the Conservative Party, the political wing of Prussian Junkerdom, panicked at any inroad into its power base. In 1892 the *Tivoli Programme* made it official Conservative policy to oppose *the often obtrusive and corrosive Jewish influence on our national life*. Open anti-Semitism was now socially respectable at the highest levels.

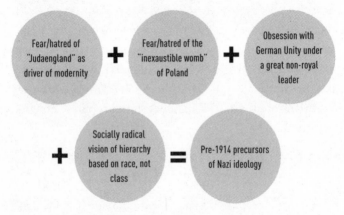

Bismarck Unleashes Anglophobia

Just as this movement was being born, Bismarck himself was hoping that a British Jew might save the Prussian Empire from war with Russia.

He was convinced that in Benjamin Disraeli, Britain at last had a real leader again—meaning, one who would stand up to Russia. A grand vision hovered before Bismarck: a global German-British alliance. And the British Conservatives saw the point.

ENGLAND, AUSTRIA, AND GERMANY.

(FROM OUR OWN CORRESPONDENT.)

VIENNA, OCT. 18 (8 P.M.).

Lord Salisbury's speech at Manchester on Friday has been received here with great satisfaction, as a guarantee of the complete understanding between England, Austria, and Germany.

The Times, October 19, 1879 (Lord Salisbury, later PM, was at this time Foreign Secretary).

It was a marriage proposal born out of geopolitical logic. Russia threatened Britain in India; it threatened Austria in the Balkans; it threatened Prussia in the Baltic. Together, the three of them could face it down anywhere on Earth.

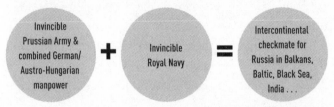

Then, in the general election of April 1880, the British shocked everyone (including Queen Victoria) by throwing Disraeli out and handing power to the liberal William Gladstone, who loathed Bismarck and vice versa.

Bismarck's plans lay in ruins. The very day the British election results became known, he sent his envoys racing to St. Petersburg in a frantic damage limitation exercise. He now switched to a deliberate policy of anglophobic colonialism. This would placate at least some of the National Liberals, who'd long demanded colonies. Bismarck had always said no to them in the past for fear of entanglements that might upset his European chess games. Now he said yes. Because now,

Uniquely, just before the 1884 Reichstag elections, Bismarck is portrayed not as a Prussian soldier but as an Imperial sailor, come to muscle in on fat John Bull's act.

distant entanglements with the Englanders were just what he wanted. They would make life hard at election time for anyone in Germany who sounded remotely pro-British—such as the Crown Prince and the new, united liberal opposition. Bismarck explained this tactic himself to the Tsar, who was amazed at such political cunning. So he unleashed the German colonial movement and made sure that its first colonies, in Africa and the South Pacific, were in areas the British regarded as their own.

There was another angle. Bismarck hoped that France and Russia might be persuaded to drop their vengeful plans for Alsace-Lorraine and the Balkans to join a new geopolitical drive at Britain's expense.

Bismarck indeed triumphed at the Reichstag elections of 1884. But nothing could break the logic that was bringing France and Russia closer: in 1885–86 the French refocused on *revanche (revenge)* against Germany, while Russian policy turned again to the Balkans, threatening Austria. Meanwhile, the price of Bismarck's anglophobic campaign was high. The Royal

Bismarck's hoped-for way out: Germany joins France and Russia in plaguing the British Lion (Gladstone).

Navy and the US Navy spontaneously made common cause against German expansion in the South Pacific: on Samoa, in 1889, it came very close to a shooting war. This was the seed of the *special relationship* between the US and the UK.

There was no natural connection at all between Tsarist Russia's ambitions in the Balkans and republican France's wish to be revenged for 1870. But because Bismarck had welded himself to Austria-Hungary in the Dual Alliance of 1879, France and Russia began to have a very obvious common interest.

By New Year's Day 1887, the constellation that would result in WWI was already visible. Waldersee, Moltke's heir apparent as head of the Prussian army, wrote in his diary that war with France was now *inevitable* and that it might become a *World War* (*Weltkrieg*). He began plotting a two-front war against both France and Russia.

Bismarck, meanwhile, plotted desperately to avoid it. He knew that the Prussian victories of 1864 (Denmark), 1866 (Austria) and 1870 (France) had depended on his diplomacy. For the sake of Prussian rule over Germany, he couldn't break the Austrian alliance of 1879, so he tried to finesse it in his secret *Re-Insurance Treaty* with Russia (1887), which promised Germany would stay neutral if Austria should attack Russia. He knew perfectly well this would never happen: the treaty was just an attempt to muddy the waters in case of war and *keep Russia off our necks for six to eight weeks* (as Bismarck's son, the Foreign

Secretary, put it) until France was beaten.

But the Prussian General Staff had come to believe its own propaganda. Wars, they thought, were won through sheer Prussian military genius and willpower. Most younger Prussian diplomats bought into the myth and were all for a showdown with Russia. The passage below isn't some impotent crackpot sounding off, but the future Imperial Chancellor, writing from the embassy in St. Petersburg to the No. 2 at the Berlin Foreign Office at a time when war seemed on the cards:

Prussian Leaders Replan Eastern Europe, December 1887
We would have to bleed the Russians to such an extent that they will be incapable of standing on their legs for twenty-five years. We must stop up Russia's resources for years to come by devastating her black earth provinces, bombarding her coastal towns, destroying her industry and commerce to the greatest possible extent. Finally, we must drive Russia back from the two seas—the Black Sea and the Baltic—which are the foundations of her great position in the world. I can only picture to myself a Russia truly and permanently weakened if it cedes those territories which lie to the west of line from Onega Bay through the Valdai Hills to the Dnieper. Such a peace—unless there were a complete internal breakdown in Russia in the event of war, which is hard to foresee to that extent—would only be enforceable if we stood on the banks of the Volga . . . we should seize the opportunity afforded us by war to drive the Poles *en masse* from our Polish provinces . . . [He goes on to describe a new, more eastern buffer-state of Poland/Ukraine, deliberately constructed for Germany to divide and rule by balancing Catholic and Orthodox inhabitants.]

Bernhard von Bülow to Friedrich von Holstein,
December 10, 1887

Only the ancient Wilhelm I's teary insistence on his royal brotherhood with the Tsar kept Europe from a vast war right then and there. He died in early 1888 and was succeeded at last by Frederick III, the great hope of the liberals—who was already mortally ill. By the end of the *year of three Kaisers*, he was gone too and the bellicose, military-loving young Kaiser Wilhelm II was on the throne.

Bismarck was all-powerful so long as he kept the trust of the Emperor, who was the only person who could sack him. But he had played power games with all the parties in the Reichstag and been loyal to none, so he could expect no backing there if he ever did lose the imperial favor. His trump card had always been to threaten the Emperor with his resignation. In 1890, the hot-headed young Wilhelm II, determined to rule as a genuine monarch, called Bismarck's bluff and let him go. There was now no civilian in Germany who could dare even enquire about, let alone challenge, the plans of the Prussian General Staff.

Germany After Bismarck: Booming but Fractured

Bismarck was gone, but he left behind a Germany ready for industrial boom.

The tariff walls he had adopted after 1880 meant that home-grown industry was protected from foreign competition. So, for example, massive publicly funded railway investment (by 1913, the Prussian State Railway was the largest single employer on earth) benefited only German companies. This close relationship between state policy and private industry gave German firms a great sense of security, helping to build the long-term view which, contemporary foreign observers noted, was very unlike the Anglo-American business model.

¹ For example, one Rhenish ironworks makes it a rule, whatever its profits, not to pay a higher dividend than 5 per cent. The rest goes into a reserve fund, and a fund for the purchase of fresh and improved plant and machinery.

From *Made in Germany* (1896) by Ernest Edwin Williams.

One thing that made reinvesting so attractive was the highly educated but poor workforce. German literacy rates were far above those in Britain or France and the working class were accustomed to military discipline and low wages. One American observer from 1902 sounds very like someone explaining China's success today:

It is probable that no civilized workman in the world would change places with the German. Few indeed work longer hours for smaller pay, eat coarser and cheaper food, live in more crowded homes, and none gives more time and substance to the government which in return hems him in with an infinite multiplicity of rules and regulations, and curtails right of free speech . . . a carpenter in the ship yards will receive about 90 cents per day for 11 hours' work. In America, a carpenter commonly expects $2.50 to $3 for 8 hours' work.

R. S. Baker, *Seen in Germany*, New York, 1902

A low-wage, low domestic consumption, state-disciplined, state-aided, tariff-protected economy needs a fat, rich consumer economy without its own tariff barriers, to buy its exports. In the 1890s, that great consumer market was Britain. Such one-sided trade relationships, though, are liable to cause friction, just as now between the US and China. To Britons, the mark *Made in Germany* already carried a chill warning of economic threat and in this first age of mass electorates, popular emotions were beginning to decide how nations lined up.

The other problem with a low-wage, export-driven economy is that your own working class, seeing no hope of any trickle-

down, is liable to become radicalized. In the 1890s, Germany became the great bastion of socialism. The Social Democratic Party's *Erfurt Programme* (1891) aimed to unite the workers for a Marxist struggle that was necessary by the laws of nature (*naturnotwendig*). It began to score major electoral success.

THE ALIEN PAUPER QUESTION.

All over the world, revolutionaries looked to Germany as the place from which the communist millennium would soon take off.

The classic way for governments to keep the working class happy is to keep staple food cheap. For booming, export-driven industrial Germany, the obvious answer was to import cheap grain from the American plains or the black earth region of Russia. And since Germany's industrialists were perfectly sane, that's indeed exactly what they wanted. But they didn't get it. Because however rich they now were, they still didn't run things. The Prussian Junkers in East Elbia did, thanks to their guaranteed domination of the Prussian Parliament, of the higher civil service, and of the army.

The East Elbian Junkers, Still in Control

Chancellors—or even a Kaiser—who attempted to tamper with the special entitlements of the rural sector risked vociferous and well-coordinated opposition . . . the

Using this political clout, the Junkers refused point blank to allow cheap food imports, for fear these would hurt their own estates. This brings us to the fatal duality at the heart of imperial Germany.

The Impossible Double Country

By the end of the 19th century, it seemed a toss-up whether English or German would be the great world culture of the 20th. Germany led the world in the latest technologies: even Britain's Royal Navy was now clad in Krupp's patent armor-plate. From the Rhine to the Dnieper, the Baltic to the Black Sea, German was the language of commerce, scholarship, and science. Yet somehow, Bismarck's successors managed to blow it.

German diplomacy from 1897 seems so irrational that great historians pore over the original documents for years, only to throw up their hands and retreat into psychology.

The German Empire's foreign and security policy was already more than heavily burdened by the enmity of France and Russia. Yet its naval armament program now sought and created an at least potential new foe in England. In terms of a calculated foreign policy, this is not rationally comprehensible.

Thomas Nipperdey, *Deutsche Geschichte 1866–1918*

But there is a perfectly rational explanation as soon as we lose the Prussian myth that Germany was *united* in 1871. It wasn't. In effect, the whole imperial German financial system was a gigantic machine for taking wealth from liberal, Catholic southwest Germany and handing it to the East Elbian Junker elite of the old, pre-1815 Prussia. The taxes paid by western

The Prussian myth:
One Reich, one Volk, one God.

German industrialists and the loaves of overpriced bread bought by western German industrial workers subsidized the agricultural estates and army jobs of the East Elbian Junkers, who despised the lot of them.

From 1898 these two Germanies, with their entirely different histories, social structures, economies, and religious arrangements, also had what amounted to separate foreign policies.

	GERMANY	EAST ELBIA
ECONOMY	Hyper-confident, booming, export-led. World leader in Second Industrial Revolution technologies: in 1913, 50% of all the world's electromagnetic devices are Made in Germany.	Tottering. Junkers crying for protection against grain imports. Flight from the East (*Ostflucht*) as German-speakers leave for better lives in West.
POLITICS (consistent through all Reichstag elections 1890–1912)	Catholic Center always largest party.	Conservative Party always largest party.

	GERMANY	EAST ELBIA
GREATEST FEAR	Anglo-Saxons. Jealous Englanders have made a tacit global anti-German alliance with US; Anglo-Saxon sea power could wipe out German fleet, exports, and colonies overnight.	Slavs. Polonization of rural East Elbia as Germans leave; Russia on the border, growing ever stronger in demography and industry.
MILITARY LOGIC	Build a fleet so mighty that Britain is forced to accept Germany as co-ruler of the world (or be beaten).	Use totality of all-German manpower to defeat Russia before it's too late.
DOMINANT SOCIAL GROUP	Wealthy burghers getting tired of doffing caps to Prussian Junkers.	Rural Junkers, clinging to top jobs in State/Army.
VIEW OF FUTURE	Imperial, industrial, colonial, bright, verging on manic. If things are run properly, modernly, not by a coterie of Junkers, the German century is coming!	Doom-laden. A grand East Prussian Junker explaining why he didn't plant an alleyway of trees to his mansion: *Why? In a hundred years, this will all be Russian.*
RELIGION	Catholics and Protestants happily coexisting, though intermarriage still rare.	German population (shrinking) almost entirely Protestant. Polish minority (growing) entirely Catholic.

The man at the helm, the half-English Kaiser Wilhelm II, perfectly expressed the split. As King of Prussia, he loved his army and so feared the Slavs that he was more and more prone to see things in terms of an upcoming *racial struggle** in Eastern Europe. Yet as German Emperor, he was instrumental in pushing for a huge new fleet under

---

* In a letter to the German shipping magnate, Albert Ballin, December 5, 1912

his immediate control, which everyone knew could only be aimed at England.

When Admiral Tirpitz's publicists began touring Germany in 1897, backed by the Kaiser himself and armed with the latest media technology (they showed some of the earliest movies in the world), millions of people fell in love with the idea of a mighty fleet. The underlying reason was simple: an imperial navy would be in effect the opposite of the Prussian army.

	Depends on	Defends	Run by	Answers to	Aimed at
NAVY	new industries	trade and colonies	modern technocrats	Empire	Britain
ARMY	rural recruits	land borders	traditional Junkers	Prussia	Russia

This explains how it was that the imperial navy had such an uncannily unifying effect. Liberals, Catholics, National Liberals, Pan-Germans, and eventually even Socialists could prove their German patriotism, yet vote against Prussian Junker rule, by backing the fleet. Doing so would also reassign some of their taxes away from the Prussian army, to be spent instead in the steelworks, laboratories, and shipyards of western Germany.

The pro-fleet movement thus became a campaign bus for everything that was radical, modern, and anti-Junker, both of the left and of the right.

Sea interests and Agrarian ambitions will be brought again into opposition with one another . . . The contradiction between Industry and the Agrarian lobby will be ever

This may sound like the analysis of a Marxist professor condemning the agricultural Junkers to the dustbin of history, but Captain (later Admiral) von Heeringen was actually head of the imperial German navy's propaganda office.

On March 26, 1898, the first great *Fleet Law* was passed in the Reichstag, and from that day onward, the Prussian-German Empire sealed its own doom by preparing for two completely different and contradictory wars at the same time. The navy toasted *The Day We Set Forth Against England* (as the 1911 song put it); the army thought only of swift victory over France followed by all-out assault on Russia. In April 1904, Britain and France buried their differences in the *Entente Cordiale*, settling colonial disputes in Africa and Southeast Asia. Soon, their generals were talking. In spite of this, the *Schlieffen Plan*, the Prussian General Staff's incredibly detailed timetable for the rapid conquest of France as the mere precursor to the great drive on Russia, was not altered by so much as a single day.

Even now, it seemed impossible that Russia and Britain, who had been in state of cold war since the Crimean War, could ever be genuine military allies. A rational German diplomacy could still have played one off against the other. But with Prussia gunning for Russia and Germany going after England, and with no one able to control this two-headed Empire, the impossible alliance between London and Moscow came about in 1908.

The apparent military-diplomatic irrationality which created the Great War was the consequence not of German unification, but of its non-unification under Prussia.

Germany: thinks it must defeat Anglo-Saxons

Prussia: thinks it must defeat Russians

World Power or Downfall

From 1908, the 10th anniversary of Bismarck's death, the Prussian royal and Junker regime was not only faced with a logically invincible coalition of Britain, France, and Russia, but was also virtually under internal siege.

On the left, the Social Democrats were booming at the polls and confidently awaiting the socialist millennium which everyone, including Lenin, believed would soon be ushered in by Germany.

Even the old, moderate liberals were growing impatient with subsidizing the Junkers, who strutted around in full uniform, armed, liable to challenge to a duel any respectable middle-class person who stared too long, or simply to cut down anyone who they considered non-duel-worthy (*satisfaktionsunfähig*) for, say, bumping into them. And they always got away with it, because as officers of the Prussian army they were tried only by their peers. One of the greatest liberals, lawyer, and politician Hugo Preuss, wrote that if Germany was ever going to be truly westernized, it needed a *definitive solution to the Junker problem.*

Rosa Luxemburg, one of the leaders of German Socialism, c. 1910. Note to modern cultural thinkers: as a radical, she has boldly raised in a public place the veil which, as a respectable woman, she naturally has attached to her hat.

On the right, Bismarck's old supporters, the National Liberals, the party of the Protestant middle classes, were anti-Junker too, but for different reasons. They wanted a modern and efficient state that was nothing to do with Western models, led by a non-royal leader who somehow knew what The People wanted: a *plebiscitary leadership democracy* said their guru, Max Weber, founder of sociology. Frowning monuments to the Iron Chancellor sprang up all over Germany. The greatest of them, which still glowers over Hamburg, already seems to come from a new, and perhaps darker era.

1906: Over 100 feet tall, a distinctly modernist Bismarck looms gigantically down over Hamburg.

It was a radical modernizer, Maximilian Harden, who in 1908 broke the sensational story that Kaiser Wilhelm's innermost Junker cabal were gay and secretly called their 49-year old sovereign *the little darling* (*das Liebchen*). Harden did it, he claimed, because this clique of unmanly Prussian aristocrats could not be trusted to defend German interests against cunning modern politicians like Edward VII of England (by now known in Germany as *Edward the Encircler*).

Wilhelm's personal regime was tottering. Outbid on the political right wing by modernizing Bismarckian nationalists, publicly accused of surrounding himself with homosexuals, terrified of red revolution, he compensated by becoming ever-more Prussian and militaristic.

Everything was at breaking point. German-language art of this era is matchlessly tense and thrilling, vibrant with wild

Bedeutsames vom englischen Besuch

„Was hast du denn da in deiner Tasche, lieber Onkel?"
„Europa, lieber Neffe!" —

The Kaiser's Prussian feudal regime is no match for Edward VII's sleek, civilian modernity: *What have you got in your pocket, dear Uncle?* asks the hapless Wilhelm II. *Europe, dear nephew,* replies the hooded-eyed Edward.

yearnings for liberation and the sense of impending catastrophe.

The Seismograph of Art, 1908–14

In visual art, the groups *Die Brücke* (*The Bridge*) in Dresden and *Der Blaue Reiter* (*The Blue Rider*) in Munich gave a home to those who fought against the stultifying Prussian academic art establishment in Berlin, from which some resigned outright (hence the name *Secessionists*). The Kaiser called their work *gutter art* (*Gossenkunst*). Stage writers pushed the boundaries of a strict censorship; composers like Gustav Mahler and Richard Strauss tried to outbid and overcome the mighty influence of Richard Wagner's doom-ridden Germanic operas by writing works of megalomaniac length and volume, with titles like *Resurrection* or *Death and Transfiguration*. The greatest writers of the era—Thomas and Heinrich Mann, Robert Musil, Franz Kafka, Rainer Maria Rilke, Stefan Georg—were almost all inspired by the ecstatic writings of Friedrich Nietzsche, who prophesied the *reevaluation of all values* (*Umwertung aller Werte*) and the coming of the *super-man* (*Übermensch*). Their heroes are often transfixed by the *frenzy of total downfall (Raserei des Unterganges)*, as Thomas Mann put it in *Death in Venice* (1912).

The Prussian Junkers felt it, too. Only war could preserve their domination. For them, it was *Weltmacht oder Untergang* (*World Power or Total Downfall*)—the title of the 1912 bestseller by the Prussian cavalry general von Bernhardi.*
At the notorious *War Council* of December 8, 1912, General von Moltke pleaded that it kickoff as soon as possible—but

---

* No single English word seems to render the full power of the German *Untergang*.

he knew he was going to have to sell Prussia's war on Russia to the German people.

> ## The War Council, December 8, 1912
> Gen. von Moltke: "I consider a war inevitable—the sooner, the better. But we should do a better job of gaining popular support for a war against Russia, as per the Kaiser's remarks." H. M. confirmed this and asked the secretary of state to use the press to work toward this end.

Anyone who thinks of the Germans as a naturally bellicose people should recall that Prussia-Germany was the only one of the continental powers in the run-up to 1914 whose elite seriously feared that if they had their war, their people might refuse to fight it.

The last recorded time Moltke repeated his mantra *the sooner the better* was June 1, 1914. On June 28, news came from Sarajevo: Archduke Franz Ferdinand, heir to the Habsburg Empire, had been assassinated by a Serbian nationalist. On July 5, 1914 Kaiser Wilhelm II gave Austria-Hungary's general staff the *blank cheque* they'd been waiting for since 1879: full Prussian military support for whatever they chose to do in sorting out their Slav problem.

The Austrians thought the Russians would back down. They didn't. The rest followed. The Kaiser tried to stop things at the last minute, but Moltke hysterically told him that any tampering with the Prussian General Staff's sacred railway timetables would be fatal. And so, just as Bismarck had predicted (having created the conditions himself) *some damn stupid thing in the Balkans* between east-facing Germans and Slavs set off the First World War.

The Breaking of Nations

Germany should have won the war. Its industry had a vital edge on the Allies, above all in cutting-edge fields. Until the British used tanks in late 1916, the Kaiser's forces were always first to get new war technologies: poison gas, flamethrowers, super heavy artillery, long-range heavy bombers (the *Zeppelins*), truly effective submarines, machine guns which could fire through aircraft propellers. While the Allied forces played technological catch-up, awful leadership created disaster after bloody disaster for them in 1914–15.

By the autumn of 1915, Prussia-Germany and Austria-Hungary indeed looked set for victory. Massive gains from the Russians meant that the *Supreme Command in the East* (*Ober Ost*) now had its very own colony, complete with currency and press bureau, and utterly outside civilian control. The ultimate aim of Prussian policy in the east hadn't changed in the 28 years since Bülow's letter to Holstein of December 1887 (see p. 124): annex a strip of once-Polish (now Russian) territory directly to Prussia, create a new Poland out of other areas currently ruled by Russia, and deport all Prussia's Poles there. From the Baltic to the Black Sea, everyone would be under open or *de facto* German rule. Or rather, Prussian rule. A memo from the Chancellor's closest advisor shows just how much the imperial elite of WWI still thought of themselves as Prussians, not Germans.

Propaganda and money from the colony of Ober-Ost.

> [We should think of] the German Empire as a limited company with a Prussian majority shareholding. Every new shareholder in the Empire reduces the majority on which Prussian hegemony within the Empire depends. Therefore: we construct around the German Empire a league of states in which the Empire has a majority shareholding, just as Prussia does within the Empire—thus giving Prussia the actual leadership within this league, too.
>
> Kurt Riezler, April 18, 1915

In late 1916, Russia, having exhausted itself in a last great offensive against the Austro-Hungarians, wanted out. The once-despised British Army had just given the German army a huge shock in the great struggle of the Somme, and was now enemy number one. The offer of a quick peace with Russia was thus a breathtaking opportunity. Chancellor Bethman Hollweg and the Kaiser himself saw the logic and wanted to give it a chance. There was only one thing no Russian could ever swallow, and that was *Ober Ost*'s plan for a vassal German Poland.

By now the true rulers of Germany were Field-Marshall Paul

von Hindenburg and General Erich Ludendorff, who'd made themselves national heroes by smashing the Russian invasion of East Prussia in 1914. A reporter from the still-neutral US, the great H. L. Mencken, witnessed their iconic status among both the public and the military: *Hindenburg remains the national hero and beau idéal; nay, almost the*

The true rulers of Germany from August 1916: Hindenburg (l.) and Ludendorff (r.).

national Messiah . . . ten of his portraits are sold to one of Wilhelm's . . . Ludendorff's hangs in every mess room; he is the god of every young lieutenant. Both these men hailed from Posen/Poznań, one of the most Polish areas of Prussia. To them, solving the Polish problem was the whole point of the war. They simply went ahead with their plans, broke off contact with Russia and on November 5, 1916 established the puppet state known as the *Kingdom of Poland*, under a theoretical German regency. Russia was outraged and, in a public announcement on December 14, 1916, cited the fact that *Germany has proclaimed the illusory independence of Poland* in vowing to continue the war. The High Command's refusal to give up, or even delay, its long-mooted Prussian plans for engineering a new Eastern Europe had thrown away a real chance of victory.

It happened again, in spades, a year later. In the west, terrible German decision-making had gratuitously created another potent enemy. The German Navy's sustained targeting of Atlantic merchant shipping with submarines (*U-boats*) outraged American opinion; the ineptitude of the Prussian State Secretary for Foreign Affairs, Arthur Zimmerman, did the rest. He approached Mexico with the near-farcical offer of an anti-American alliance. British intelligence intercepted it and gleefully informed Washington. The US was dragged into a war which very many of its citizens and politicians would gladly have sidestepped.

In the east though, things were looking good for Germany. Ludendorff deliberately allowed Lenin to pass through Germany into Russia in a sealed train, hoping to infect Russia with revolution. It worked perfectly. In October 1917, Lenin's *Bolsheviks* seized power, and Russia's new leader sued for peace so that he could consolidate his grasp. Faced with a huge new enemy in the west and a collapsing foe in the east, any sensible German leadership would have done a reasonable deal with Russia straight away, freeing up fifty-plus divisions for the Western Front.

Prussia remakes the East: The Treaty of Brest Litovsk, March 3, 1918.

For Ludendorff, though, just beating Russia wasn't enough. On February 13, 1918, he announced his dizzily vast new plan: smash the new Bolshevik regime and restore the Romanov Tsars as mere clients of Prussia. Those fifty-plus divisions were sent charging off eastward again, pursuing a millennial fantasy of final victory in the ancient German-Slav conflict beyond the Elbe, even as thousands of American troops began to arrive at the Western Front.

On the maps it looked like a gigantic triumph, and was trumpeted as such to the German people. But it meant less than nothing. A million men were still in the east, policing these vast but useless conquests, when the British army decisively cracked the German lines in France, on August 8, 1918:

Hindenburg on the Battle of Amiens, August 8, 1918
A strong English tank attack had met with immediate success . . . The tanks, which were faster than hitherto, had surprised Divisional Staffs in their headquarters and torn up the telephone lines which communicated with the battle front... The wildest rumors began to spread in our lines. It was said that masses of English cavalry were already far in rear of the foremost German infantry lines. Some of the men lost their nerve . . . I had no illusions about the political effects of our defeat on August 8.

It was Prussian strategy that lost the war. Scornful of Anglo-Saxon warmaking and obsessed with remodeling northeastern Europe, it condemned Germany to defeat in the West.

Repeated Prussian underestimation of "Anglo-Saxon" readiness/ability to fight in West **+** Prussian obsession with epochal restructuring of German-Slav power relations in East **=** Germany loses war

The End of Prussia-Germany

The *political effects* Hindenburg feared were indeed spectacular. By now the British blockade, combined with terrible
harvests and a lack of manpower to get the crops in, had
reduced many Germans to near starvation.

According to a report entitled *Hunger*, issued by The
School Care Committee Section of the Berlin Teachers'
Union, "The moral sense was in many cases deadened
by the animal fight for existence. The feelings of physical pain, hunger and thirst, physical exhaustion and
enervation, dominated nearly all sensations, and often
influenced desire and action." As food became more
scarce, German civilians began acting out primal instincts
to feed themselves, and in many cases this need dominated their entire lives. According to the same report,
morals, cultural norms, and laws were often blatantly
disregarded as millions sought to obtain what they and
their families needed to survive. This often caused otherwise law-abiding citizens to engage in illicit acts such
as theft, cheating, or assaulting other citizens in their
never ending quest to feed themselves.

*The British Blockade During World War I: The Weapon of
Deprivation*, David A. Janicki, Enquiries 2014, Vol. 6

The one thing that sustained people was the hope of eventual
victory. And in August 1918, most Germans still genuinely
thought they were going to win. Even in September 1918, the
Imperial government could still raise most of its expenditure by selling allegedly guaranteed high-interest war bonds
to its own trusting people. The German people might not
like the East Elbian Junkers but, knowing only what strict

censorship allowed them to know, they still believed their warlords invincible in battle.*

When the truth was revealed—that the German army's morale and Ludendorff's nerves were both finished—it came like a thunderclap. On September 29, 1918, Ludendorff suddenly told the Kaiser they needed to form a new government because *the military catastrophe could not be put off much longer.* On October 3, 1918, Hindenburg confirmed this to a shocked Reichstag. Now, quite deliberately, the generals who'd run Germany for the past two years handed power to the civilians just in time for them to, as Ludendorff put it, *ladle out the soup* (i.e. take the blame).

Kiel, November 3, 1918: rebellious sailors hail the *socialist republic.*

The moment the myth of Prussian military invincibility died, Germany rose up. Violent rebellions and mutinies shook the country, most famously on November 3–4 when sailors in Kiel refused to set sail for a suicidal last battle with the Royal Navy.

On November 9, the Kaiser fled the country. His last Chancellor, Prince Maximilian von Baden, simply handed over the keys, without any proper legal formalities, to Friedrich Ebert, leader of the moderate Social Democrats (who

---

* It takes some effort now to recall how easy it was for governments to control a media which still consisted only of newspapers and celluloid newsreels.

had supported the war effort). Later that same day, the Republic was proclaimed from a balcony of the Reichstag—and was then proclaimed again, in a rival address from the back of a truck in the Lustgarten park, by Karl Liebknecht, leader of the so-called *Spartacists*, the left-wing Social Democrats, who drew inspiration from the revolution in Russia.

In the chaos, only one thing was certain. After less than fifty years, the Prussian Empire of 1871 was history.

The Doomed Republic

The new Chancellor, Ebert, charged Hugo Preuss, the man who two decades earlier had called for *a definitive solution to the Junker problem*, with devising a new constitution for Germany to set before the National Assembly. Preuss looked consciously to western constitutional traditions. Parliament (the Reichstag) and the President were to balance one another, and to be directly elected by the whole country—men and women—in separate elections, on the American model. Preuss also planned to break Prussia up within his new Germany. In January 1919, a National Assembly was elected to agree the constitution. With Berlin racked by street fighting, it convened instead at the National Theatre in the culturally famed city some 180 miles to the south—Weimar—hence the republic's name.

Preuss worked desperately to get his draft constitution agreed before peace was simply dictated to a beaten Germany. If the new system appeared to have been imposed by the Allies, it would, he knew, be fatally compromised. This need for speed led him to drop his plans for partitioning Prussia. But his efforts were in vain: on June 28, 1919, before the deliberations were finished, the *Treaty of Versailles* was signed under duress by Germany.

The Treaty of Versailles

The essence of this vast and complex treaty was that Germany had to (i) accept the blame for starting the war (ii) pay the Allies huge reparations (iii) give up all its colonies outside Europe (iv) hand over various territories to various European neighbors and (v) have its armed forces limited to a size which could never again be a threat to anyone.

Germany after Versailles.

By the time Ebert signed off Preuss's new constitution on August 15, it was all too easy for monarchists and militarists to claim—as they immediately did—that the democratic Weimar Republic was just another facet of this treaty: a foreign way of doing things, forced on Germany at gunpoint by the western powers. The fact that Preuss was a Jew made him and his work an even easier target.

Preuss was determined (like the liberals of 1848) to westernize Prussia within Germany; but some western Germans thought Prussia a hopeless case, and wanted to break with it entirely. Konrad Adenauer, the Catholic Center Party's Mayor of Cologne, formally demanded an end to what he saw as the Prussian occupation.

> Prussia has ruled Germany, and lorded over the peoples of western Germany, whose whole way of thinking is essentially sympathetic to the peoples of the Entente. If Prussia were to be divided up, and the western regions of Germany to league together, it would make it impossible for Germany to be ruled over by the spirit of the East.
>
> Konrad Adenauer, February 1, 1919

Adenauer tried again in October 1923, lobbying at the highest level for French support for a West German Confederation (as he called it). Like the Archbishops who in 1804 invited Napoleon to *cross the Rhine to drive out the barbarians*, he never doubted that his Germany had more in common with France than with Prussia.

Prussia at Bay

Prussia had always been different; now it became rabid. It had lost a swathe of land the size of Belgium to the despised Poles. It had also lost its psychological anchors.

In this frontier zone, life had been ordered since 1525 around unchanging principles. The ruler of Prussia was absolute; the Junkers were his unquestioned lieutenants, virtual princes on their own estates; and the Lord of the Land was also Head of the Church, the spiritual as well as temporal guardian of his people against the Catholic Poles around them. All that was gone. Who would protect and guide them now? President Ebert, leader of the godless socialists, backed by southwestern papists, who had already signed away so much of Prussia to Poland?

It seemed the end for the Junkers. Gone was the royal Prussia which had for generations guaranteed them all the top posts in state and army; gone, too, that three-tiered electoral gerrymandering which had enabled them to dominate the Prussian Parliament. Now their votes counted for no more than those of their peasantry, their titles officially counted for nothing, and their jobs were gone. Some of them were ready to make common cause with the anti-Semitic rabble-rousers they'd scorned as noisy trash before the war. Many of them simply kept right on fighting that war.

The war had not ended in East Elbia. The place was, as ever, different. Fighting there went on during and after the signing of the Versailles Treaty. Entire divisions of the Free Corps, artillery and all, fought over Posen/ Poznań and Silesia with the Poles. They actually tried to conquer the Baltic States. When one of their leaders, Hans von Manteuffel, fell during the storming of Riga in May 1919, his funeral rites self-consciously harked back to the Teutonic Knights—as did the propaganda of the newly-formed *German National People's Party* (*DNVP*).

"Save the East"
(from Poles and Socialists)

The *DNVP* was founded in 1919 as an umbrella group for former members of the Junker-run Conservative Party or of the army-funded *Fatherland Party*, for Pan-Germans, anti-Semites and suchlike. It allowed no Jews in. It was monarchist, thoroughly based in East Elbia, and almost entirely Protestant.

The politicians it identified as enemies were publicly lambasted as being traitors in the pay of Jewish and/or Catholic interests; several were assassinated by men with clear links to the party. By 1924, the

DNVP National Convention, December 1924.

DNVP was the second largest party in the Reichstag. But its almost-fifth share of the national vote came overwhelmingly from East Elbian Prussia.

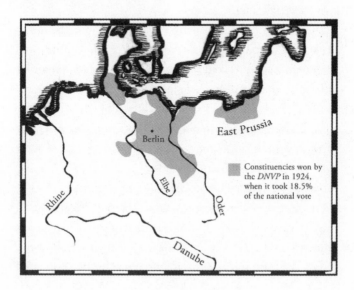

Constituencies won by the *DNVP* in 1924, when it took 18.5% of the national vote

As long as the 1871 version of Germany remained a single state, the monocultural otherness of East Elbia distorted everything. No wonder that Adenauer, having failed to split western Germany off, was said to close the curtains in his train compartment whenever he passed eastward across the Elbe, muttering, *Here we go, Asia again* (*Schon wieder Asien*).

Prussia and Russia: The Secret Brotherhood

The Versailles Treaty reduced the German army to a peace-time limit of 100,000 men, but, crucially, it didn't alter who chose them.

General Hans von Seeckt, who was left in charge, was an arch-Junker—his father had governed the now-lost region of Posen/Poznań—and he made sure that the right sort of people got the few thousand officers' postings left. Every insider knew, for example, that the inoffensively modern-sounding *Ninth Infantry* considered itself heir to the exclusive Prussian Imperial Guard.

The result was that the German army after 1919, the *Reichswehr*, was proportionally even more a Prussian Junker one than before 1914, packed tight with highly decorated junior officers of ancient military name who would never get promotion unless the army grew vastly again. They had seen their beloved Prussia republicanized and amputated in favor of their former underlings, the Poles. The smoke of WWI had scarcely cleared before their leader, Seeckt, was looking forward to the day when this would be put right.

His remedy was to be a revival of the old Prussia-Russia axis. It may seem deeply unlikely that monarchist Junker officers could agree on anything with Russian Bolsheviks. In fact, beneath the superficial differences in their supposed ideologies, they shared profound cultural affinities: a scornful hatred of the democratic West and its alleged decadence; the worship of sheer, brute force; a cultic veneration for militarized state power; and, most importantly of all, a loathing of the reborn Poland.

As early as April 1920, one of Lenin's diplomats in Berlin was already suggesting the possibility of *combining the German Army and the Red Army* for a joint war on Poland. Von Seeckt was enthusiastic. To him Russia was still Russia, whether it was a monarchy or a Soviet republic, and he believed that Russia and Prussia could bury their differences, as they had throughout the 19th century, in an anti-Polish alliance.

The existence of Poland is intolerable and incompatible with Germany's vital interests. She must disappear and will do so through her own inner weakness and through Russia—with our help. Poland is even more intolerable for Russia than for ourselves; Russia can never tolerate Poland . . . the attainment of this objective must be one of the firmest guiding principles of German policy, as it is capable of achievement—but only through Russia or with her help.

Hans von Seeckt, 1922

Lenin himself realized that the radicalized Junkers after WWI were a new sort of animal. He called them *a curious type of reactionary revolutionary* and was happy to do business with them. At Rapallo in 1922, Weimar Germany and Soviet Russia publicly came to terms on reparations. But unknown to the world, the Reichswehr and the Red Army also did a deal which allowed Seeckt's men to lease various training camps deep in Russia, far from prying Western eyes. In these secret facilities, both armies could train in the use of modern weapons, especially tanks, which were forbidden to Germany by the Versailles Treaty.

Allied against the West: an early German-made tank during joint Soviet-German testing at the secret Kama training ground in Kazan, 200 miles east of Moscow, 1931. Many German officers were impressed by the discipline and morale of the Red Army, and by its central status in the new Soviet state: *From the mid-1920s onwards, German army leaders developed and propagated new social conceptions of a militarist kind, tending towards a fusion of the military and civilian sectors and ultimately a totalitarian military state* (F. L. Carsten, *The Reichswehr and Politics: 1918–33*).

Even as the hard right plotted with Moscow against the western-style republic, so did the hard left. With hunger and unemployment rampant, and with demobbed soldiers everywhere, the German communists attempted to imitate Lenin's coup in the *Spartacist Uprising* of January 1919 and the *March Action* of 1920.

Since the new government had no reliable forces of its own as yet, it had to turn to the Free Corps, led by unpurged Prussian generals. They crushed the red rioters, but then tried to take over themselves in the so-called *Kapp Putsch* of March 1920 (recent research suggests that the obscure civil servant-turned-journalist Wolfgang Kapp was in reality just a front-man for ex-General Ludendorff himself). One of the units which led it was the *Erhardt Brigade*, already sporting the swastika on their helmets.

Swastikas on our helmets/Black-white-red our flag/We are called the Ehrhardt Brigade/The Ehrhardt Brigade/smashes all it meets/Woe to you, woe to you, worker scum. The song was later taken over, as were many Ehrhardt members, by the Nazis: they simply changed the words *Brigade Ehrhardt* to *Sturmabteilung Hitler.*

The Kapp Putsch was defeated by a general strike and by the refusal of officials to do its bidding. But this peaceful, democratic resistance was turned by the Communists into another armed left-wing uprising, this time in the industrial heartlands of the Ruhr. The government suppressed this, using more Free Corps.

The moderates of the so-called *Weimar Coalition* (which basically meant the Social Democrats and the Catholic Center Party) were thus trapped from the start between forces of the extreme left and right, both of whom wanted to overthrow the new democracy by physical force.

The republic was desperately in need of a solid, central, peaceable block of citizenry. Unfortunately, that very group was now hit by a new trauma.

The Death of Money

From 1921 to 1923 hyperinflation on a unique scale wiped out millions of people's life savings. The root cause was the bonds Imperial Germany had used to fund the war. Essentially, the government had borrowed from its own people at unrealistically generous interest rates. The plan had been to pay this money back by, in effect, robbing conquered peoples. That was now impossible.

The new Weimar Republic was thereby saddled at birth with state debts roughly proportionate to those of Greece in 2013 (approx. 175% of GDP). But there was no one to bail it out. The Allies wanted a new Germany, but they also insisted that it should pay for the old Germany's war. On top of that huge inherited debt, the republic now had vast reparations bills to the victors, which had to be settled in hard currency.

Germany was too fragile politically for massive tax rises to be an option, or for any national, patriotic appeal to stand a chance. So the government started printing Reichsmarks wildly, both to pay back its debts to its own people and to buy up foreign currency. The more they printed, the more the buying power of the Reichsmark sank, the more money they had to print, the more the Reichsmark sank . . .

Catastrophic inflation spread from the foreign exchanges to the streets of Germany. In 1914, a dollar had cost 4.2 Reichsmarks; by January 1921, it was 191.80. The final blow that tipped the currency right over the edge came when the French occupied the vital industrial Ruhr Valley region in January 1923, to enforce delivery of reparations, mainly in the form of coal. The government in Berlin encouraged passive resistance by declaring that strikes were a patriotic act and promising to pay strikers' wages. This meant printing even more paper money just as industrial production (and therefore, the tax take) was crippled. By November 1923, a single US dollar notionally cost 4.2 trillion Reichsmarks.

Things were stabilized in 1924 by a new currency backed with hard assets: the *Rentenmark*. But by then, millions of hard-saving, government-trusting, middle-class Germans had seen their lives' savings (including those supposedly cast-iron, state-

Remember: the German billion = the US trillion.

backed war bonds) entirely wiped out. This hit a vital sector of civil society hardest. If you were a farmer, a landlord, or an industrialist, the underlying value of your property wasn't in the end affected; if you worked for day wages and had no savings, nothing really changed either. But if you were one of the huge swathe of once-prosperous Germans who didn't own physical assets but had always saved hard and believed in the state—civil servants, doctors, teachers, white-collar workers, shopkeepers, university lecturers, and so on—you were left feeling abandoned by the new republic.

In Munich, an ex-corporal, Adolf Hitler, who'd initially been paid out of secret army funds to agitate against left-wing ex-comrades, found he had a particular gift for expressing the feelings of those who believed that the new order had betrayed them.

The Rise of the Nazis

The southern city of Munich is inextricably associated with the Nazis, even though in the last free elections Hitler didn't even break 25% there (as we'll see). However, after WWI, a unique set of circumstances combined to make the Bavarian capital briefly a haven for extreme right-wingers.

Revolutionary soldiers patrol Munich, 1919.

For five months of 1919, a Soviet-style republic terrified Munich's middle-class inhabitants. Initially peaceful, it was radicalized by the communist *Factory and Soldiers' Council*. This appealed directly to Lenin for help and ended up executing alleged spies without trial, before being itself viciously suppressed by the right-wing Free Corps. In the brutalized city, the old hatred of Prussia transformed into a loathing of the left-wing capital, which was now dubbed *Red Berlin*. The authorities in Munich from 1920 to 1924, some of whom wanted full independence, were determined to frustrate *Red Berlin* at every turn, even if that meant refusing to hand over political murderers who'd fled there.

This was the atmosphere in which Hitler entered politics. The young Nazi party (of which Hitler was not the founder) was only one of dozens of hard right groups sheltering in Munich in 1920. Its policies, its language, and even its flag were simply a remix from the Pan-German/National Protestant fringe before 1914. As Hitler swiftly became its *de facto* leader, what made it stand out was its deliberate copying of the street-fighting style and the modern-seeming politicking of the new, Lenin-inspired left.

Hitler and Lenin: Dark Modernism

Just as von Seeckt's Prussian Junker army, radicalized by defeat, found much to agree on with the Red Army, so Hitler's ideas were closer to Lenin's than to any traditional European conservatism. Both Lenin and Hitler appealed to perverted versions of that great 19th-century liberal ideology (as seen in Hegel, Marx, and Darwin): the idea of of progress-through-struggle-to-utopia. This is a notion fundamentally at odds with conservative thought. In both Leninism and Nazism, that pre-1914 ideological DNA had been deformed and hardened by the industrial slaughter of the Great War. Hitler and Lenin cared as little as a WWI general had for the fate of any individual. They defined Progress solely in terms of the Masses, be they *the Workers* or *the German Race,* and were happy to condemn—literally, to condemn to death—anyone they regarded as a block to that Progress. It's no coincidence that both were fascinated by *Fordism*, the cult of mechanized modernity centered on the high-tech guru of the new production-line era, Henry Ford.*

Yet at the same time, Hitler managed to persuade people that all he really wanted was to bring back the good old days. Perhaps the best way to show the lie at the heart of Nazism is

---

* Ford was himself a rabid anti-Semite who actually helped fund the young Nazi party. In gratitude and admiration, Hitler had Ford's portrait hung in his own office from 1922–24.

through architecture. Below is the famous *Bauhaus building* of 1925. It is a hymn to the religion of modernism, built by radical, left-leaning architects who claimed that such impersonal, industrial, factory-like living would improve life for The People.

The next picture is the Nazis' *Reich Aviation Office* of a decade later. It used the same factory-like lines and modern materials—steel and concrete—as the Bauhaus, but with a purely decorative overlay of cod-classical details.

By plastering his radical modernism over with superficial conservatism, Hitler could seem all things to all people. He claimed he wanted only to restore Germany's past glory, yet his

men acted like Communists, calling themselves a movement, pouring out bile on reactionaries, throwing leaflets from speeding trucks and picking fights in the streets.

The Nazis soon caught the eye of Captain Ernst Röhm, a war-disfigured army staff officer whose nickname in Munich was *the machine gun king* because he controlled access to the Bavarian army's secret arms-dumps. He liked this new little party so much that he eventually joined it and became head of its paramilitary wing, the *Sturmabteilung*, or SA (Assault Division).

Röhm was vital as a broker of contacts to the old Prussian elite. This, too, was central to Nazi success. In 1922–24, Hitler was very much second fiddle on the right to General Luden-dorff, who'd effectively been boss of Germany in 1917–18. Being close to Ludendorff gave Hitler priceless respectability and wealthy sponsors. It also changed his own thinking in a fateful way. It was only now that the arch-Prussian idea of colonial *Living Space (Lebensraum)* in the east became a central part of Hitler's ideology—it wasn't mentioned in the original 1920 Nazi manifesto at all.

Pre-WWI "national Protestant" thought + Radicalized post-WWI modernism + Superficial conservatism + Traditional Prussian geopolitics = Nazi Ideology

On November 9, 1923, Hitler and Ludendorff staged an attempted coup—the *Beer Hall Putsch*—in Munich, intending afterward to march on Berlin. It was a debacle which should have ended Hitler's career then and there. But instead of a punishment fitting the crime of armed high treason, anti-Berlin judges in Bavaria gave him a year's fortress arrest (*Festungshaft*). This was usually reserved for army officers who'd broken the civilian law but not the military code of honor. A non-sentence like this was a distinction for ex-corporal Hitler, not a punishment at all.

Still, at the time, it did seem to be the end for him. With hyperinflation mastered by currency reform and the *Dawes Plan* delivering US loans to Germany rather like an early-21st-century EU bailout, people were ready to give the new republic a chance. Even the DNVP eventually took part in the governing coalition. Weimar Berlin became the intellectual and artistic powerhouse of Europe.

Weimar Culture

For the first time since 1819, German culture was free of Prussian absolutism and of the *despotism ameliorated by incompetence* (Victor Adler) of Austria, too. It was now a Western-style land at last, in which no one was conscripted, women could vote, gay nightlife could flourish openly and Jews were finally able to take up full posts in universities and politics. American culture was delightedly embraced—and transformed. Brecht and Weill's *Threepenny Opera* and *Mahagonny* turned jazz music and a popular, accessible feel into a new theatrical form. Visual art took inspiration from posters and street scenes. Novels like *Berlin Alexanderplatz* by Alfred Döblin (1929) hymned big-city life and tried to imitate its frantic rhythms. Above all, German film went to uncanny, erotic, and imaginative places where even Hollywood had never been.

Freed from Prussia by the military and political triumph of the West, Germany was once again at the very heart of things.

Metropolis (1927)
Nosferatu (1922) and
The Blue Angel (1930)

It would be easy to suppose in hindsight, or in the sad light of recent European politics, that all this excitement must have been limited to a metropolitan elite in Berlin and probably repelled everyone else. History, though, says otherwise. The Reichstag election of 1928 gave the center-left SPD, the party most strongly identified with the new Republic, its best result since the heady days of 1919, leaving it far and away the biggest party. The party of small-town resentment and snarling protest against Americanization and liberalism, the Nazis, scored a paltry 2.8%.

Yet two years later, of course, they were the biggest single party, and by 1933 they were in power. The question is how this—   1928

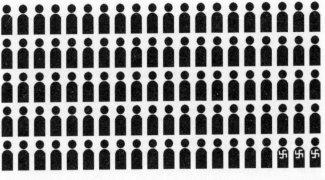

—turns to this: 1933

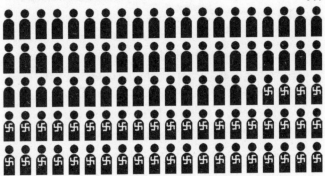

The Nazi Breakthrough

The obvious explanation is the 1929 Crash, which froze the US economy, and hence the vital lines of American credit to Germany. Unemployment soared to 1.6 million (September 1931) and then to 6 million (January 1933). The system was in meltdown. But Hitler was only able to benefit so much from this because by then, he'd already been gifted a unique national profile.

It was the *DNVP* that made him. The party could call on proud old names and wealthy donors, but it was so decidedly Prussian—and hence, Protestant—that it had never appealed much even to right-wing voters in other regions of Germany. The new leader, media tycoon, and former Krupp board member Alfred Hugenberg, decided that the Nazis were really just a smaller, rougher version of the *DNVP* with a useful hard core of grassroots activists. Thugs, yes, but our thugs. What if the hard-talking, modern-seeming, but essentially conservative brownshirts could deliver some votes from the rest of Germany, leaving their social superiors, the top-hatted *DNVP*, natural rulers of East Elbia, as the real power in the land? This delusion persisted right up to the day Franz von Papen, the last Chancellor before Hitler, gave his famous-last-words assurance to his colleagues on January 4, 1933: *We've hired Hitler.*

The *DNVP*–Nazi alliance of 1928 was such a gift to Hitler because Hugenberg controlled huge swathes of the press and almost all the cinema newsreels. Hitler understood the power of simple imagery in the mass-media age, and made sure he looked the part in every reel. The non-media-savvy, top-hatted and imperial-uniformed old men were seen chatting and waving, but Hitler made tough love to the cameras as the burning-eyed New Man. By the time Wall Street imploded in 1929, he had become a national figure—but crucially, one who wasn't identified with the Junkers and *The System*.

A cross in no. 10 is a vote for the *National Socialist German Workers Party* (*Hitler Movement*).

When the Crash came, some Germans went for a charismatic individual who'd been on all the screens and had fanatically loyal followers but who was unsullied by government and promised simple things, right now. It was all about the man, not the party. Uniquely, the Nazis had their leader's name as a personal subtitle on Reichstag voting slips from 1928 onward: *Hitlerbewegung* (*Hitler movement*).

But to *which* Germans did this man and his movement appeal? The answer, as so often, can be found in the lines of religion and topography that still bisected the nation.

Who Voted for Hitler?

Let's imagine that you are shown the blank back of a photograph. This photograph is of a random German of voting age in 1928. Your task, for a large prize, is to guess whether this person will switch to the Nazis by 1933.

By just guessing no, you'd have a slightly better than 50/50 chance, because the Nazi vote in 1933 was 43.9%. But you are allowed to ask a single yes/no question to improve your odds.

So, what will you ask? Will you try to narrow down their age, their class, their gender, their education, their job?

Here's the greatest modern electoral scholar in Germany, coming to the conclusion, after many pages of tables and statistics, that only one question would be of any real help. The answer seems to surprise him, because it's so simple.

The Only Question Worth Asking

It is clear that the key compositional predictor of the Nazi vote in Weimar Germany is the Protestant ratio of the local population . . . Hitler's strongholds were clearly in the Lutheran countryside; the greatest factor is almost always the confessional makeup of the constituency, measured by the proportion of Catholic voters . . . The confessional factor proves itself astonishingly robust and relatively constant; it seems to have had a significantly greater influence on electoral results in the towns and communities of the German Reich than the various indicators of class.

Jurgen W. Falter *Die Wahlen des Jahres 1932–33 und der Aufstieg totalitärer Parteien*

Germany's biggest news magazine boiled it down like this:

In July 1932, only 17% of Nazi voters came from predominantly Catholic regions.

Der Spiegel, January 29, 2008

It is worth hammering this point home: if you're trying to forecast whether a random German voter from 1928 will switch to Hitler, asking whether they are rich or poor, town or country, educated or not, man or woman, and so on will scarcely help at all. The only question really worth asking is whether they are Catholic or Protestant.

This is why it's vital to challenge the Prussian myth of German Unification in 1871. Because it's not as if Catholics and Protestants were (or are) equally distributed across Germany. In Germany, your religion isn't just a matter of personal preference or theological conviction. It's a sign of which historical Germany you come from. So the only meaningful way to track the Nazi breakthrough (or lack of it) is on maps.

Here's the Nazi vote in 1930. Suddenly, from 2.8%, they had soared to 18.3% nationally, making them the second largest party and stealing all the headlines. But *where* exactly did that takeoff occur?

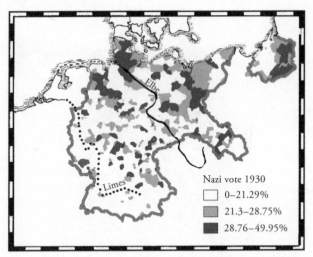

Source: *The Electoral Geography of Weimar Germany*, Prof John O'Loughlin, University of Colorado Institute of Behavioral Science.

Put the line of the Roman *limes* across this picture, and the line of the Elbe. Within the Roman Empire of 100 AD, there is virtually nowhere the Nazis broke 20% and large swathes where they didn't even make 15% (so much for the idea that Bavaria was the Nazi homeland). Extend that to the border of Otto the Great's empire in 940 AD (the Elbe), to include what social geographers call middle Germany (*Mitteldeutschland*) and you find some places where the Nazis made serious ground, but many where they made very little. And then there's East Elbia, with solid blocks of constituencies already voting over 30% Nazi in 1930. The great Nazi breakthrough at national level was overwhelmingly due to East Elbian voters.

It was the same story two years later, in July 1932, when the Nazis scored their highest vote in a genuinely free election and became easily the largest single party in the Reichstag (though without an overall majority):

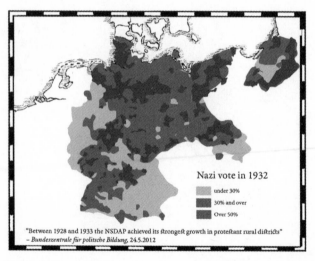

Nazi vote in 1932

- under 30%
- 30% and over
- Over 50%

"Between 1928 and 1933 the NSDAP achieved its strongest growth in protestant rural districts"
– *Bundeszentrale für politsche Bildung*, 24.5.2012

Almost all of East Elbia voted over 40% for Hitler in July 1932, and much of it gave him over 50%. The comparison with the map of the Catholic population is stunning in its clarity, being almost exactly a reverse image:

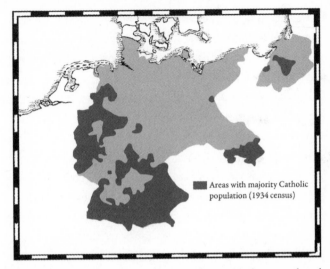

Areas with majority Catholic population (1934 census)

Then came the final, fatal election of 1933. Hitler was already in power. He'd become Chancellor on January 30, 1933, after machinations at President von Hindenburg's East Prussian estate. He was notionally in coalition with the *DNVP*, led by Vice-Chancellor von Papen, who'd promised he could control Hitler. While the SA thugs—50,000 of them now on the state payroll—made normal electioneering almost impossible for the left and liberals, Nazi propaganda, with the whole governmental machine behind it, made a major pitch for the middle ground.

Nazi electoral posters, 1933. *Left*: "The Reich will never be destroyed so long as you are united and faithful" (the line is from a famous statue of Wilhelm I erected in 1897). *Right*: "The Field Marshal and the Corporal: fight with us for peace and equal rights."

The great new theme was Hitler's respectability. After all, the old, beloved warrior, Hindenburg, had turned to him in Germany's hour of need!

At the height of the campaign, on February 27, a Dutch communist, Marinus van der Lubbe, set fire to the Reichstag. Whether van der Lubbe was directed by the Dutch communists, a radical lone wolf with a history of mental illness, or the fall guy for a Nazi plot is still debated by historians. However the fire happened, it was a huge boost for Hitler.

And so we get to election day, March 5, 1933: there has never been a more tempting time for voters to swallow Hitler's claim that the Nazis are really just a rougher version of the traditional right wing, and have to be tough to stop the Communists from taking over. Every Weimar Reichstag election so far has been followed by horse trading and coalition building, but March 5, 1933 is more like a straight referendum or a presidential election, because this time everyone knows in advance exactly what their vote means. A cross for the Nazis or the *DNVP* says, *yes, I want Hitler to stay in power*. A cross for anyone else at all says, *no, I want Hitler out*. Time to choose.

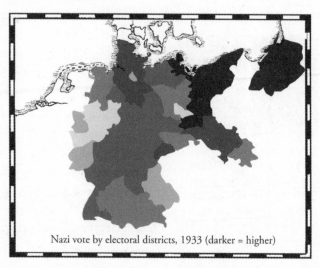

Nazi vote by electoral districts, 1933 (darker = higher)

In many areas within the Roman *limes* of 100 AD, Hitler fails to break 35%, even at this stage. The average here overall is well under 40%. Even with the whole state apparatus behind him, even with Hindenburg's blessing and the great scare campaign after the Reichstag fire, even after a campaign tailored to make him seem as normal as possible, Hitler has failed to take the west and south of Germany. In fact, only two constituencies within the bounds of Otto the Great's Empire of 940 AD (Ost-Hanover and Chemnitz-Zwickau) give Hitler a majority—and they both lie right at its eastern limits, on the western banks of the Elbe.

For that river, as ever, is the great fault line in German history. Things are different east of it, as they have been for a thousand years. Here, Hitler smashes it outside Berlin (always a political island within East Elbia). The only three constituencies in the whole of Germany where the Nazis get over 55% are all here. Hitler has clearly failed to win a majority in the west, but this big East Elbian vote pushes him up to 43.9% nationally.

Hitler still needs the *DNVP*, the party of the Junkers. It brings 7.9% of the votes. These come, as ever, disproportionately from East Elbia. If you put the Nazi and *DNVP* vote together, East Elbia outside Berlin has gone approx. 60% for the Hitler Coalition. It's this regional anomaly alone which gives the Nazi/DNVP coalition a bare majority in the Reichstag: 51.9%.

Immediately, Hitler demands an *Enabling Act* (*Ermächtigungsgesetz*). This is a device in the Weimar constitution which allows the Chancellor to govern without parliament in time of alleged crisis. Hitler needs a 66% supermajority to maintain a fiction of legality. As opposition MPs enter the Reichstag on March 23, 1933, they run a jeering gauntlet of uniformed Nazi thugs. The Social Democrats bravely vote no. The Center Party decides, after agonized debate, that if it votes against a 51.9% national mandate, Germany's Catholics will be cast once again as traitors to the will of the people, and suffer a vicious new *Kulturkampf.* Hitler gets his super-majority, and democracy in Germany ends.

Who exactly killed it? If all Germany had voted like the Rhineland, Swabia, and Bavaria between 1928–33, Hitler would never have become Chancellor, let alone dictator. East Elbian votes gave him his breakthrough in 1930, then confirmed him in 1933. No East Elbia, no Führer; it's as simple as that.

Ever since the British handed Prussia the Rhineland in 1814, the whole of Germany had been slowly dragged and deformed toward an East Elbian agenda. In 1933, defeated and amputated but still undead, East Elbia finally took all Germany with it into the abyss.

Was der König – der Fürst – der Feldmarschall – rettete und einigte
eroberte, formte, verteidigte, der Soldat.

That which the King conquered—the Prince formed—the Field Marshal defended—the Soldier saved and united

Hitler's Careful Days

At first Hitler was extremely careful to pose as a normal leader—normal, that is, within the Prussian tradition.

The great danger now came from his own radical wing. Ernst Röhm, his old friend and leader of the party's paramilitary wing, the millions-strong SA, wanted a genuine Nazi revolution in German society, right now. In particular, he planned to absorb the elitist, conservative army, as laid down in point 22 of the original 1920 Nazi program.

The army was outraged. Its leader, Junker defense minister General Werner von Blomberg, was all for the Nazis; in February 1934 he personally ensured that the very few Wehrmacht officers with any Jewish ancestry (all of them Christians) were sacked. But he would not accept subordination of the Junker army to the thugs of the SA.

Hitler pleaded and lobbied with both sides. Neither would yield. At last, he was directly ordered to sort things out by Reich President Hindenburg, who was 87 years old and declining fast, but still had the constitutional power to sack the Chancellor. On board the brand-new battleship *Deutschland* on April 9, 1934, Hitler struck a deal with Blomberg: he would tame the SA and vastly expand the army if the generals promised to back him as total leader of Germany after Hindenburg's death. To fulfill the bargain, Röhm and between 150 and 200 SA leaders were killed on the *Night of the Long Knives* (June 30, 1934).

President Hindenburg publicly congratulated his Chancellor. Hitler knew that he'd been entirely in the hands of the generals during the crisis, and hurried to thank them in public. He announced that the army was to be the *sole bearer of arms in the land* and even said that it was all right if any individual soldier didn't *find his way to us*. This meant that you could officially still rise in the armed forces (as many did) without ever joining the Nazi party. It was a unique concession, and meant that the senior echelons of the German Army could still delude themselves that they were somehow above the dirty business of politics.

The Junker officer caste were delighted with the deal. Hitler, it turned out, was just the sort of civilian leader they'd more or less openly longed for ever since 1919. On the very day the ancient Hindenburg died (August 2, 1934), Blomberg introduced a new oath without even being asked by Hitler, never mind ordered: soldiers now swore *unconditional loyalty* to the *Führer of the German Reich and People, Adolf Hitler.*

Prussia Squared

Between 1871 and 1918, Prussia had tried, with little success, to impose on all Germany its signature features: a militarized society, state worship, leader adoration, zombie-like obedience (*Cadavergehörsam)* and scar-faced, armed young Junkers swaggering about in uniform, looking for trouble, virtually beyond the law. After 1934, the Nazi state was far better at it.

The alleged new elite of race deliberately mimicked the Junkers' arrogance, their clipped, parade-ground speech and their readiness to use personal violence if crossed. When the SS (*Schützstaffel*) set up its own cadet camps, it called them *SS Junker Schools.* One of the textbooks used in them taught that *cutlery should be held only with the fingers, not in the entire hand.* For this was social radicalism: so-called *aryan certificates* replaced family trees of noble lineage as the way to advancement. No matter how ancient your title, if you had any Jews in your family, you were in trouble—whereas any chicken farmer or bank clerk with proper German blood and a party card was now invited to act in the way the Junkers always had. SS functionaries who had never been near a horse aped the riding breeches of old cavalry regiments; their black uniforms (often proudly tailored by Hugo Boss) and skull device were taken straight from the exclusive 1st Imperial Hussar Life Guards.

Kaiser Wilhelm (l.) in the uniform of the Death's Head Hussars; his eldest son, Wilhelm (r.), with SS chief Heinrich Himmler.

This new would-be aristocracy simply made the law up as they went along, confident that so long as they were being radical, they were *working towards the Führer*, as the expression had it. But an aristocracy must have someone to lord it over. All so-called pure-blood Germans were now said to be equally part of the *Folk Community*. Of course, there were *traitors to the people*—leftists and liberals—but with them imprisoned, exiled, or terrified into silence, the Nazis needed to find, or invent, non-Germans in Germany. Without the friendless Jews, the Master Race would have had no one to be master of until 1939. Anti-Semitism, which had been made into a political movement by Prussian radicals, and made respectable by Prussian conservatives, became the very glue of the peacetime Nazi state.

Hitler, Unopposed

Only the spinelessness of the other powers allowed this vile regime to survive and grow. After 1919, America was clearly the most powerful nation on earth. If it had remained committed to an active role in the world, no German leader would have believed he could revise the result of WWI by force. Instead, the US failed to step up to the international plate, opting instead for isolationism. Russia had been traumatized by revolution and famine, and was now in the grip of Stalin's murderous *Great Terror*. Stalin was terrified of provoking the German attack he knew would some day come. An exhausted Britain simply couldn't believe that anyone in Germany actually wanted another war; until 1938, its leaders stayed fatuously convinced that if they treated Germany fairly—generously—Hitler would be satisfied. France was even more scarred by war and was so torn by internal left-right political conflict that many Frenchmen feared the German army less than their own communists.

This non-opposition handed Hitler triumph after triumph, when any real resistance would have soon finished him.

1936: Remilitarization of the Rhineland & the Berlin Olympics

Under the Versailles Treaty of 1919, no German forces could be based in the Rhineland. Hitler simply went in. He admitted at the time that the German army was as yet completely unready for any confrontation. The slightest Franco-British military opposition would have stopped him dead. Britain and France did nothing, and Hitler's popularity in Germany reached new heights. For the 1936 Berlin Olympics, Hitler ordered violence against the Jews to be briefly stopped, so that he could

By 1936, the Nazi State was widely seen as an acceptable partner.

showcase the Nazi State to the world. This was the high point of the regime's international acceptance.

1938: Anschluss (*Union*) *with Austria*

In 1919, the victorious Allies had declared that nations like the Poles and Czechs had the right to live as united peoples. Hitler argued: why not the Germans too? There was no international opposition whatever when the German army went into Austria. Hitler was greeted ecstatically in Vienna. His popularity rose higher still.

1938: *Munich Agreement*

The ancient German minorities in the Austrian kingdom of Bohemia (under Austrian rule until 1919) had always wanted to leave the new Czecholslovakia and join with Germany. Now, Hitler demanded the unification of this German-speaking *Sudetenland* region with the Fatherland. The Czechs were ready to fight. They filled the mountains facing Germany with some of the best forts, tanks, and anti-tank guns on earth. Many German generals believed that if France and Britain backed the Czechs, Germany was sure to lose. Some were ready to kill Hitler rather than face certain defeat, and they even told Britain so. But Britain was too scared of Germany's allegedly invincible airpower. At the infamous Munich Conference (September 30, 1938), British Prime Minister Neville Chamberlain sold Czechoslovakia out to save peace: it was made to give up the Sudetenland without a fight. President Roosevelt cabled him: *Good man.*

Hitler had achieved total unification of all the Germans without a fight. He was now untouchably popular among the people, and among junior army officers. The generals abandoned their plot.

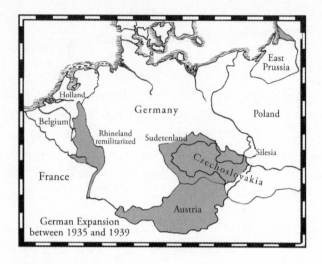

German Expansion
between 1935 and 1939

The Real Hitler Steps Forward

After Munich, Hitler at last felt free to do whatever he wanted. He no longer needed to pose as conservative. What he really wanted became clear on the night before Luther's birthday, November 10, 1938. The *Kristallnacht* pogrom unleashed Nazi thugs to smash and burn Jewish premises and synagogues all over Germany. The Nazis' Propaganda Minister, Josef Goebbels, crowed that *the radical view has triumphed.*

This *radical view* suffused Hitler's major speech to the Reichstag on January 18, 1939. It's justly notorious for prophesying the *annihilation (Vernichtung) of the Jewish race in Europe.* But Hitler also promised the *Vernichtung* of any priest who stood against him. As for the Junkers who had helped him into power, he promised the Nazis would *brush aside the efforts of dying social classes to set themselves apart.*

Anyone could now see that Nazism had nothing whatever to do with traditional conservatism. There's a common argument that the Nazi State was radicalized by the nature of war itself (this idea unites apologists for Nazism with pacifists who believe that no war can ever be right). But the truth is the other way round: Hitler well knew—he said so himself several times—that he would only be able to do truly radical things under wartime conditions, when any opposition could be immediately silenced.

In March 1939, he dropped all pretense and invaded what was left of Czechoslovakia, before adding a slice of semi-German Lithuania to East Prussia. Then came the deal that amazed the world: the Nazi-Soviet pact to partition Poland.

It seemed incredible that Hitler and Stalin could unite. But in fact, it had been the norm throughout the 19th century for Prussia and then Prussia-Germany to find common ground with Russia in (and only in) a shared wish to keep Poland abolished. More recently, there had been those secret military agreements between von Seeckt and the Bolsheviks. By carving up Poland to square Russia, Hitler was acting like every Prussian leader since Frederick the Great.

With Russia onside, he could have his war. And that meant that he could start being truly radical at last. On September 1, 1939, he gave two orders. One was to attack Poland; the other was the green light to fully implement a secret program for the purification of the German race. There's no doubt whatever that Hitler personally ordered this program. He thought it so important, and knew it was so radical, that in a very rare move he provided a signed authority to the killers.

The Holocaust

It's tempting to print an entire page in solid black and just go to sit in some blessed garden, trying to forget what happened among the railway sidings and birch forests of *Mitteleuropa*.

Here, if anywhere, is something too awful for rational discussion or comprehension. But we can't leave it at that.

> **Death in the Gas Chambers**
> At first, some of the victims seemed to believe that it really was just a shower they were taking. Others began at the last moment to resist and shout out . . . after an interval, operatives in gas masks opened the doors. Terrible sights normally greeted them . . . the operatives who attended to the crematorium, sometimes called burners, were also responsible for taking the corpses to the ovens . . . patients with gold teeth had been identified by a cross against their names and these teeth were taken out and delivered to the administrators, to be melted down to fine gold.
>
> *Landeszentrale für politische Bildung*
> *Baden-Württemberg,* 2000

The people in the description above are not Jews in Auschwitz, but handicapped Germans being killed in Germany in the so-called *T4 Aktion* of late 1939 to August 1941.

During this period, despite massacres by gun and bayonet in Poland and, from June 1941, in occupied Russia, the Jews in Germany itself were not yet being systematically murdered, and no special facilities had yet been built to kill them in. The unique features of the Holocaust were developed in the earlier purge of allegedly *life unworthy* (*lebensunwert*) Germans.

This prequel to Auschwitz was stopped by the last vestige of western civilization left in Nazi Germany. Himmler had complained that it was impossible to keep the murders secret enough within Germany. As the head office of the SS put it on June 6, 1939, *one can declare with certainty that the Lutheran part of the population has a better understanding of the struggle and mission of the SS than the Catholic part.* There was still a line which the Catholic Church would not, could not cross.

On August 3, 1941, Cardinal von Galen of Münster spoke so openly and powerfully against the *T4 Aktion* that his sermon was later printed and dropped as propaganda on German cities by Britain's RAF.

There are sacred obligations of conscience from which no one has the power to release us and which we must fulfill even if it costs us our lives ... the doctrine is being followed, according to which one may destroy so-called "worthless life," that is, kill innocent people if one considers that their lives are of no further value for the nation and the state.

Cardinal Clemens August Graf von Galen

It was an act of extraordinary courage. Von Galen was kept under virtual house arrest until the end of the war, but he survived (unlike three of his priests, who were beheaded) because, even now, the Nazis had to think twice before murdering popular Catholic establishment figures from the least Nazified part of Germany.

"If any action were taken against the Bishop," Goebbels apparently said, "the population of Münster, and for that matter the whole of Westphalia, could be written off for the duration of the war." Hitler agreed that inaction was the wisest course, though he privately vowed to have Galen's head after the war.

Nicholas Stargardt, *The German War*

Galen's bravery, and the Nazis' awareness of popular feeling in Catholic areas, meant that the production-line mass-killing of the handicapped was stopped in August 1941.

By then, around 70,000 German men, women and children had already been murdered, many of them gassed en masse and then cremated in specially-built facilities. Everything was set up for the Jews. But *T4* had shown the Nazis that, even in wartime, they couldn't just start killing people wholesale within Germany.

The SS needed somewhere no turbulent priests would interfere, where their work could be kept really secret, where European civilization had already ceased to exist. By late 1941, with Poland and swathes of western Russia in their hands, they had just the place. When, on January 20, 1942, senior Nazi

officialdom gathered to coordinate strategies for the eradication of Europe's Jews (the so-called *Endlösung*, or Final Solution) at the Wannsee Conference, the SS No. 2 Reinhard Heydrich spoke pointedly of *our new prospects in the East*. In that conquered and shattered wasteland, his words implied, no one was going to object.

House of Darkness: The villa where the Wannsee Conference decided on the *Final Solution*. You leave the museum there with the relief of someone waking from a terrible dream. Then you remember it was all true.

Heydrich could be confident because there had already been appalling massacres of Jews there by the end of 1941, with full cooperation from the army. The following order was not from the SS, but from from an aristocratic Prussian field marshal, to all the men under his command:

> In the eastern theater . . . the soldier must learn fully to appreciate the necessity for the severe but just retribution that must be meted out to the subhuman species of Jewry . . . This is the only way we can remain true to our historic mission *to free the German people once and for all* from the Jewish-Asiatic menace.
>
> Field Marshal Walter von Reichenau,
> general order to 6th Army, October 10, 1941

This area had, as we've seen, been earmarked for decades by scheming Prussian militarists as a future colony. Add in radical Nazism and you had a self-fulfilling prophecy. First, you claimed that this East was a naturally state-less, culture-less place (conveniently forgetting that Prussia had been born and raised under the throne of Poland and that only Russia had saved it from extinction at the hands of Napoleon in 1807). Then you made it so, by systematically demolishing all local institutions, murdering any potential leaders, and ruling by force applied in the most arbitrary and brutal way. You thus created a hideous colonial non-order in which the worst elements of the local population would naturally rise. Only then were the conditions right for the true unfolding of Nazi radicalism:

> It was only with the conquest of Eastern Europe that Hitler had the opportunity to create a truly anarchic society in which expropriation, murder, and extermination could be practiced without restraint . . . the impact of Nazi mass killings in other countries depended largely on how far the state and its institutions had managed to survive. Thus most Jews escaped being murdered in Belgium and Denmark, where the institutions of the state,

In the apocalyptic world the Nazis had created beyond East
Prussia, there was no restraint. And so the *T4 Aktion* was
now exported from Germany, fully tested: the same people
in charge, the same killing techniques, the same bureaucratic
euphemisms, the same secrecy, even the same money-making
schemes. At Auschwitz, Treblinka, Majdenek, and Sobibor
the Jews were, like the German handicapped but in far vaster
numbers, treated as Darwinian antimatter to be annihilated
in the name of Progress.

The Holocaust is the unadulterated expression of that dark
modernism whose theories made people solely a mass and Progress the sole category of value—and whose practices abolished
all the carefully constructed barriers by which western civilization had contained and marginalized individual brutality. It
required no trumped-up charges and allowed for no mitigation.
Europe's Jews were treated as *vermin* because—in a tradition
we can trace directly back to those new-style Prussian Anti-
Semites of 1879—they were allegedly the natural enemies of
"German-ness." Despite the crimes of Stalin and Mao, the
Holocaust has no parallel.

The Holocaust Memorial
beside the Brandenburg
Gate in Berlin today.

Why the Nazis Lost

In June 1940, Hitler had no remote challenger left in Europe, or within Germany. Stalin was his ally, and Britain seemed sure to give in soon. Even when Britain failed to collapse or come to terms, it had little offensive capability. Hitler could easily have consolidated his hold on all Europe without any serious interference. Instead, he attacked Russia.

He gave various reasons for this: that it would deprive Britain of her last hope; that it would win him oil-fields; that Russia would attack first if he didn't. The best guess, though, is that he did so because he genuinely believed it would be a repeat of Ludendorff's easy 1918 drive eastward, but this time with no Western Front to spoil things. In Hitler's mind, as in that of the Prussian leaders of 1914–18, the whole war was really about settling things once and for all in the East. Few German generals in June 1941 (almost all of whom had fought in the east as junior officers in WWI and/or with the *Freikorps*) doubted they would win. The attack on Russia was a thoroughly Prussian decision.

The result was that by the end of 1941, the *Wehrmacht* was locked into a fatal war of attrition with the numerically unbeatable Red Army while the *Afrika Corps* was toe-to-toe with a distinctly unbeaten British Empire in Egypt. Yet on December 11, 1941, Hitler gratuitously declared war on America as well. His decision-making may appear familiar:

Ideological underestimation of "Anglo-Saxon" readiness/ability to fight **+** Obsession with smashing Russia right out of Europe **=** Germany loses war again

Since late 1941 a few officers, led by Henning von Tresckow, had been planning to overthrow Hitler. Tresckow narrowly failed to kill him in March 1943 when a bomb he'd placed in Hitler's plane failed to explode. To plot against Hitler at the height of his power was truly heroic.

Soon, though, opposing Hitler began to seem mere common sense. The stunning German loss of Stalingrad (January 1943) meant that Hitler badly needed a big victory; his scorn for the Anglo-Saxon democracies made him believe that he could gain one against the British and the as-yet untested US Army in North Africa. Ignoring the pleas of his ace general, Rommel, he pumped first-rate troops into Tunisia; the defeat that followed (May 1943) was almost as bad from the German army's point of view as Stalingrad itself.* When the colossal tank battle at Kursk (July 1943) was won by the Russians, the writing was on the wall for anyone with eyes to see. Secret opposition to Hitler now grew rapidly, led by the charismatic Klaus von Stauffenberg.

Among the plotters were many men of undoubted bravery and moral intent, but their tardiness left even the best of them open to the charge that they wouldn't have acted if Hitler had kept on winning. Many wanted peace in the west only in order to fight on in the east. Even those who were truly idealistic, like Stauffenberg, had trouble realizing just how thoroughly beaten Germany already was, or how hard other nations might find it to see the difference between a

---

* It hasn't gone down in the German national memory like Stalingrad because the 130,000 men who surrendered to the Anglo-Americans all lived, whereas the 90,000 captured by the Russians nearly all died.

Good Junker and a Bad Nazi.* Their organization was so poor that the future Chancellor, Konrad Adenauer, refused to join, asking *have you ever met a general with a clever face?*

On July 20, 1944, in the East Prussian HQ known as the *Wolf's Lair* (*Wolfsschanze*), Stauffenberg primed his bomb at the last minute in conditions of almost unbelievable stress before leaving it in a briefcase right next to Hitler and then leaving the conference on a pretext. As he was clearing security to leave the Wolf's Lair, he heard the bomb go off and was certain the dictator was dead.

Even so, the plotters had no confidence in their own legitimacy. Instead of telling the world what they'd done and why, they bizarrely announced that they were only taking power because Hitler had been killed by the treacherous SS.

In fact, he had survived: the bomb had only been half as powerful as planned, and Hitler was shielded by a massive oak conference table. Since the plotters had omitted to cut or secure communications between the Wolf's Lair and Berlin, Hitler was able to speak personally to army major Otto-Ernst Remer, who promptly had all the plotters arrested. Inexplicably, Stauffenberg and his comrades were unwilling to make an open fight of it, despite all being armed, even when they realized they were doomed. This rebellion of aristocratic soldiers was quashed with hardly a gun shot to show ordinary Berliners that anything big was going on.

---

* Yet the idea that a de-Nazified Germany might fight on against Stalin wasn't completely farfetched. Before the end of 1944, Churchill himself commissioned *Operation Unthinkable* to investigate the feasibility of a surprise UK/US attack on Russia in 1945; the report was ordered to assume that the Anglo-Americans would be aided by German troops. The British Army declared the idea a non-starter.

Hitler took hideous vengeance on anyone connected to the plotters. Auschwitz worked on. The German armies crumbled in Normandy and Russia. Germany's cities were bombed almost at will by the USAF and RAF. Yet industry reached its peak war production only in August 1944: Hitler still had resources and he still controlled large areas.

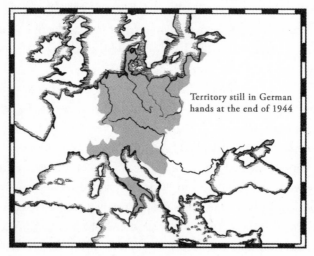

Territory still in German hands at the end of 1944

He could have thrown everything at the Russians, to try to save Germany from invasion by the allegedly subhuman Slavs. But he still believed, against all the evidence but in a thoroughly Prussian tradition, that the Anglo-Saxons, being decadent and democratic, would crack if hit hard enough. So instead of prioritizing fighter aircraft, Hitler demanded that vast efforts be devoted to firing masterpieces of technology at London. These *V-Weapons* were the world's first large military rockets, far in advance of anything the Allies possessed.

In the brutal equation of total war, though, they were incredibly cost-ineffective: the 9,000 V-1s and 1,100 V-2s fired at

Launch of a V-2, the world's first ballistic missile

Britain, all packed with non-reusable cutting-edge technology, killed on average fewer than one person each. Meanwhile, Hitler's last truly effective strike force—over 400,000 men, with more than a thousand tanks or self-propelled guns, backed by everything the Luftwaffe had left—vainly dashed itself against the US Army in the *Battle of the Bulge* (December to January 1944–45) on the Franco-German border. The surprised and outnumbered Americans had to give ground, but held out in vital towns like Bastogne until reinforcements and massive airpower halted the Germans, then drove them back.

Once this gamble had failed, there was no way to hold back the Russians. They charged vengefully across the North European Plain and into Germany. Hitler forbade any evacuation plans, condemning the women of East Elbia and Berlin to suffer *the greatest phenomenon of mass rape in history* (Anthony Beevor), which led tens of thousands of victims to commit suicide.

The Russian and American forces met up—where else would West and East meet up?—on the Elbe. Hitler shot himself dead on April 30. On May 8, 1945 the war in Europe ended.

Old Borders Restored

Since the German armies had resisted bitterly right to the end, the Allies naturally expected trouble from a post-war resistance movement. Instead, they found themselves in a land where the entire system seemed to have collapsed overnight. One of Germany's greatest modern writers recalls it thus:

> Feigtmaier, the local Nazi boss, a man feared and greeted with deep respect two days ago, now stood in his brown uniform and swept the streets, leaping up onto the pavement, sprayed with dirt, as the jeeps sped narrowly past him . . . Men had to pull off their caps and raise their hats to the English soldiers, the victors . . . Men who until just now had been greeted in clipped tones, who'd held forth with thunderous commands, suddenly whispered that they hadn't known anything about it all.
>
> Uwe Timm, *Am Beispiel meines Bruders*

This time has gone down in German history books as *Zero Hour* (*die Stunde Null*), the moment everything stopped and had to be started up again, from scratch.

The victors handed West Prussia to Poland, divided East Prussia between Poland and Russia, gave Alsace-Lorraine

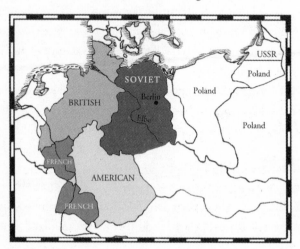

back to France and split the rest of Germany into pre-agreed zones of military rule.

Germany east of the Oder was gone forever, but no one intended the rest to stay divided for long. At Potsdam (July/August 1945) the Allies declared their aim to partially de-industrialize Germany, thoroughly de-Nazify it, and then *to prepare for the eventual reconstruction of German political life on a democratic basis and for eventual peaceful cooperation in international life by Germany. To this end, all democratic political parties with rights of assembly and of public discussion shall be allowed and encouraged throughout Germany.*

It was very soon obvious that the Russians were going to do things their own way. On the very day Hitler committed suicide, Stalin flew in a ready-made client administration of obedient German Communists from Moscow. At this time, he was not planning for a divided Germany: he wanted a united one kept permanently weak and poor. So he tried to force the pace at which industrial plants and raw materials were seized as reparations, and demanded a share in the governance of the British zone, where most of German industry was concentrated.

The British, though, were desperate to get Germany working again because they just couldn't afford to feed a non-working industrial Rhine/Ruhr as well as their own people. By 1946, Britain was forced to ration bread at home, something which had never happened during the war. Broke and desperate, it proposed—or begged for—a union with the American zone. The Americans were also determined that Germany should be set going again. Stalin's plan to keep it poor was, they believed, merely a prelude to a communist takeover. The best safeguard against that was capitalist prosperity. Unlike in 1919, the US now stepped up.

We thought we could stay out of Europe's wars, and we lost interest in the affairs of Europe. That did not keep us from being forced into a second world war. We will not again make that mistake . . . The US has formally announced that it is its intention to unify the economy of its own zone with any or all of the other zones willing to participate in the unification. So far only the British Government has agreed to let its zone participate. We deeply appreciate their cooperation.

US Secretary of State James Byrnes, Stuttgart, September 6, 1946

As the former Allies lined up into rival Anglo-American and Russian camps, things took on their own, unplanned momentum. Churchill made his *Iron Curtain* speech in 1946; the *Truman Doctrine* (March 12, 1947) stated that *it must be the policy of the US to support free peoples who are resisting attempted subjugation by armed minorities or by outside pressures.* In June 1947, the organs of the US and British zones were formally united in Frankfurt, the ancient alternative capital to Berlin, creating the *bizone.* The same month, the Marshall Plan to rebuild Europe was announced: it provided massive American loans aimed at reconstructing European economies (and thereby, Europe's capacity to buy American goods). The Russians rejected it out of hand; the French accepted and joined their zone of Germany with the US/UK bizone, making it a *trizone.*

Suddenly, without anyone having intended it, Europe looked uncannily as it had done in 814 AD, at Charlemagne's death. The Elbe was the border in the north, with Slav culture dominant beyond it, and even west of the Elbe further south.

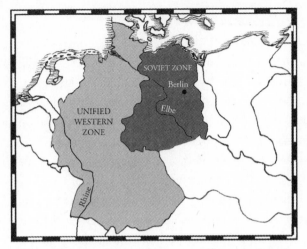

"When the dividing line was drawn across Europe at the end of World War 2, it is as if Stalin, Churchill and Roosevelt had studied carefully the status quo of the age of Charlemagne on the 1130th anniversary of his death." (Andre Gunder Frank, *Economic and Political Weekly*, Nov. 14, 1992)

The first priority for the West was getting its part of Germany going again. The old Reichsmark (RM) was by now so distrusted that it had been practically replaced in daily life by cigarettes. Without a functioning currency, there could be no recovery.

In late 1947, under *Operation Bird Dog*, new banknotes were printed secretly in America. They were shipped to Germany between February and April 1948 in 23,000 falsely marked crates, which were then hidden away in the cellars of the former *Reichsbank* in Frankfurt. The trouble was, no one could agree on how best to introduce this brand-new money.

In desperation, the Americans turned to those who really ought to understand the German economy and people: the Germans themselves. They, it turned out, had a ready-made plan up their sleeves.

The Economic Non-Miracle

Back in 1943, SS chief Heinrich Himmler had secretly ordered a panel of experts under *SS-Gruppenführer* Otto Ohlendorf (later hanged by the allies for leading a death squad) to prepare for a return to normal free-market rules once the war was won. Ohlendorf's panel included the free-market theoretician, Ludwig Erhard, the future Chancellor of West Germany (1963–66), and top banker Karl Blessing, later President of the Bundesbank (1958–69).

They soon saw that the Nazi economy was kept running only by wild printing of money. Throughout the war there had been nothing remotely like luxuries in the German shops to buy, and the price and supply of basic goods had been strictly controlled. All the spare cash had therefore been been placed safely on ice, in people's bank accounts. The Germans had in effect been forced to save hard for a decade, whether they wanted to or not. But what would happen when the controls were taken off? Erhard, Blessing, and their colleagues had no doubt about the answer: if there were no vassal economies who could be forced to accept overvalued Reichsmarks at gunpoint (as the French were from 1940–44) uncontrollable inflation would be inevitable.

Erhard's solution was radical. He suggested wiping out the overhang of paper money by abolishing the Reichsmark and introducing a brand-new currency—to be called the *Deutsche Mark*—at an exchange rate of 15:1 for private savers. Business assets, though, would be converted at 1:1, minus a purely cosmetic capital levy to make things look fair. Thus the troublesome cash savings of ordinary people would be virtually destroyed, but business capital preserved.

Since this whole idea was based on the treasonable assumption that Final Victory might not, in fact, be forthcoming, it was quietly shelved in 1944. But in 1948, with the Western allies desperate to get the German economy motoring again, the time was ripe for it.

The 1944 Plan Is Implemented in 1948

Erhard and his colleagues take their old plans out of the drawer . . . On April 20, 1948, a heavily guarded bus with opaque windows brings them to the air base at Rothwesten near Kassel. There, after weeks of persuasion, the German experts get the representatives of the Allies to go along with their concept: on June 20, 1948, small savers lose almost everything, whereas owners of shares and material goods lose almost nothing . . . Erhard's policy has one aim and one aim only: to support businesses in building up their capital. This he sees as the royal road to dynamic growth.

Handelsblatt, June 25, 2006

Rival economies like France and Britain couldn't have even dared dream about so extreme a pro-business fix. Their people would never have stood for it. It was only possible in the Germany of 1948 because the ordinary citizens saw nothing but rubble around them and were glad just to be alive and free.

At the time few people realized that the endless wreckage was almost all of homes, not businesses. The Anglo-American bomber war on Germany's cities had killed hundreds of thousands of civilians, many of them in the least Nazi areas of Germany, but only 6.5% of factory machinery was a total write-off in May 1945. German industry was still a giant—and well-used to swift improvisation. In 1948, it just needed to be woken up.

Without waiting for Allied permission, Erhard now went the whole free market hog and abolished all rationing and price controls. His exchanges with the US authorities have gone down in legend:

> *US Colonel:* How dare you relax our rationing system when there's a widespread food shortage?

> *Erhard:* But, Herr Colonel, I have not relaxed rationing; I have abolished it! Now, the only coupon people need is the Deutschmark. And they'll work hard to get those Deutschmarks, you just wait and see!

It worked. Every German of this generation remembers how almost overnight, the shops were full again and the factories at work.

This apparent miracle was nothing of the kind. The *trizone* now had a hard currency with a fixed exchange rate highly favorable to exports. Business capital had been preserved by Erhard's plan. There was a skilled and educated workforce, boosted by millions of instantly assimilable refugees from East Elbia and the Sudetenland, glad to be alive, and ready to work for low wages. Most machinery still worked. And to top it all off, Marshall Aid was coming on tap as well. It all added up to the greatest and most business-friendly bailout ever.

> Here's the core. German public debt in 1944 amounted to 379 billion Reichsmarks, roughly four times Germany's 1938 GDP. Currency reform under the auspices of the US Army in 1948 wiped out this debt. To Zero . . . From 1947 to 1952, the Marshall Plan bought West Germany a foreign debt holiday . . . That makes 465 billion Reichsmarks/Deutschmarks of canceled debt, still not including all deferred interest payments . . . Does that beat Greece? You bet.
>
> Professor Albert Ritschl, in *The Economist*, June 25, 2012

With conditions so favorable, it's really no wonder, let alone an economic miracle (*Wirtschaftswunder*), that western Germany's entrepreneurs were quickly ready to start making money again.

The True Unification—Goodbye to Berlin?

Everyone was suddenly looking to the future. But how could the country move on morally and politically, when any surviving business must, by definition, have at least made its peace with the Nazi regime? How could you cure a nation almost half of whose doctors had been Nazi party members? How could you reeducate a nation in which, for ten years, all university lecturers had worked alongside colleagues who taught *racial theory*? The answer was simple, whether you were Truman or Stalin: a veil of forgetfulness was allowed to settle over all but the very worst offenders.

Konrad Adenauer, above all, was determined to fast-forward things. In June 1948, the Russians responded to Erhard's new Deutschmark by blockading West Berlin, forcing the Allies to supply the city by plane for almost a year in the *Berlin Airlift*. Adenauer used the near-war hostility between them as the space where he could realize his life's ambition of a genuinely west-facing Germany. Bonn was narrowly chosen over Frankfurt as the provisional capital and on May 24, 1949, the Basic Law (*Grundgesetz*) was promulgated. On August 14, 1949, the 73-year-old Adenauer became the first Chancellor of the *Bundesrepublik*, which he so dominated until 1963 that those years became known as the *Adenauer era*.

Adenauer's Germany looked very like the proposed Roman Germania, and Charlemagne's German empire, and Napoleon's Confederation of the Rhine. It had a buffer zone between it and the Poles, no point of contact with the Russians, and only a short border with the Czechs.

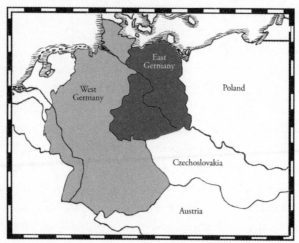

The so-called unification of 1871 had been unmade by the union, at last, of almost all Germany west of the Elbe.

Adenauer made *integration with the West* (*Westintegration*) the cornerstone of his politics. He was so single-minded in this that, during one famous debate in November 1949 the Social Democrats shouted him down as *the Allies' Chancellor.* They'd have shouted louder if they'd known what he was really thinking.

On December 1, 1955, the British High Commissioner to Germany, Sir Ivone Kirkpatrick, sent a memorandum to the Prime Minister marked *Top Secret:*

What Konrad Adenauer Really Wanted

The German Ambassador told me yesterday that he wished to make a particularly confidential communication to me . . . Dr. Adenauer had no confidence in the German people. He was terrified that when he disappeared from the scene, a future German government might do a deal with Russia at the German expense. Consequently, he felt that the integration of Western Germany with the West was more important than the unification of Germany. He wished us to know that he would bend all his energies to achieving this . . . it would of course be quite disastrous to his political position if the views which he had expressed to me with such frankness ever became known in Germany.

In other words, Adenauer simply didn't believe that a re-united Germany, with Berlin as its capital, to stay "bound to the West."

His own West Germany was indeed fitting smoothly in. In 1954 it won the Soccer World Cup; in 1955, rearmed, it became a member of NATO, the US-led western military alliance; in 1957, the Treaty of Rome created the EEC, ancestor of the EU, with Adenauer's close ally, the lawyer and diplomat Walter Hallstein, as first President of the

Commission. It really was back to the future, as a great American sociologist noted at the time:

> A comparison of the appropriate maps shows that the area of Charlemagne's empire around 814 AD, and that of the six countries presently belonging to the EEC are nearly identical . . . Such a high degree of similarity cannot be dismissed as a freakish coincidence.
>
> Hugo O. Engelmann, *The European Empire: From Charlemagne to the Current Market*, in *Social Forces*, May 1962, Vol. 14, p.297

Just how far Adenauer would have gone, given the chance, has only recently been revealed. Berlin had been shared amongst the Allies in 1945 as a separate zone. When the Russians set up their own puppet state, known as the GDR (German Democratic Republic) in 1949, the three western zones of Berlin became a heavily garrisoned western anomaly deep within the eastern bloc. During the crisis caused by the building of the Berlin Wall (1961), Adenauer made a top secret proposal to the Americans: rather than defend West Berlin, they should freely abandon the West's sole foothold in old Prussia.

> Adenauer wanted the US to offer the Soviets a swap in secret negotiations: West Berlin for the state of Thuringia as well as parts of Saxony and Mecklenburg. He made the suggestion to Secretary of State Rusk a few days before the construction of the Wall started . . . The US administration took the idea seriously.
>
> *Der Spiegel* online, August 15, 2011

But things were too fixed now. The Berlin Wall was up, and the GDR was accepted as a fact. So we'd better take a look at what was going on there.

The GDR, or The Very-Shortest History of East Elbia

East Germany didn't become different because of the Russian occupation of 1945–89; the Russians occupied the place because it had always been different.

Otto the Great invaded across the Elbe in 935 AD; the Slavs threw the Germans back out in 983 AD; the Germans tried again in 1147 and over the next two centuries they largely (but never completely) succeeded in supplanting the Slavs up to the river Oder. The Teutonic Knights went further until the Poles smashed them in 1410. Prussia was born under Polish suzerainty as an act of revolt again Rome in 1525, rose to fame in battle against Sweden, was made a great power by victories between the Elbe and the Oder, then saved from abolition by the Tsar in 1807. The fatal inability of the western Germans to unite allowed Prussia to conquer them after a single great battle on the Elbe in 1866. Prussia smashed France in 1870; it thereafter dragooned the Germans into providing manpower and money for its bid(s) to settle the 1,000-year struggle with the Slavs. That struggle ended in 1945 with part of East Elbia lost forever and what was left, between Elbe and Oder, a helpless colony of Russia.

With the creation of the GDR, this rump East Elbia formally became what it had always really been: the odd German-speaking man out in a Slavic Eastern Europe. Until the wall went up in 1961, the East Germans—above all, the young and educated—undertook a new *Ostflucht* to West Germany at an average rate of about 200,000 year on year, about the same rate as in the *Ostflucht* from the 1850s onward. If Russia's clients hadn't built and maintained a deadly barrier to stop the fugitives in the meantime, by 1989 there would have been hardly any Germans left beyond the Elbe.

Those who stayed were at the mercy of the *Stasi* (State Security) apparatus. As well as 90,000 full-time employees, the Stasi could call on 200,000 so-called *informal coworkers*. But what made the Stasi more pervasive even than the Nazis' *Gestapo* was the readiness of countless lower-level *information providers* to help it for the pettiest of rewards. They denounced friends, colleagues, teammates, even family members. A word from anyone could ruin your career, shut university to you, put you in prison, or lose you your children.

The Stasi was widely regarded as the most repressive and effective state security organization in the world, a fact dealt with by some East Germans with bitter humor. In one joke, Mossad, the CIA, and the Stasi are all tasked with identifying skeletal remains, but only the Stasi succeeds—by extracting a confession. It was also singularly effective at counter-espionage, placing a mole in West German Chancellor Willy Brandt's office, which caused Brandt's resignation in 1974 when it was discovered. Yet, like all East German institutions, it was subject to Soviet masters, and it fell apart with everything else when the Wall came down.

Pól Ó Dochartaigh, author of
Germans and Jews Since the Holocaust

Liberal West Germans, and many on the European and British left, seemed determined not to see the reality of the GDR. Otherwise sane economists accepted blatant fabrications about its

GDP; well-meaning politicians eagerly sought out evidence of its rulers' good intentions; quite intelligent sociologists claimed that, though naturally not perfect, it was a state somehow less materialistic and more communal than West Germany.

Chronic Myopia

The *Guardian* journalist Jonathan Steele concluded in 1977 that the German Democratic Republic was "a presentable model of the kind of authoritarian welfare states which Eastern European nations have now become." Even self-styled "realist" conservatives talked about communist East Germany in tones very different from those they adopt today. Back then, the word "Stasi" barely crossed their lips.

Timothy Garton Ash, *New York Review of Books*, 2007

Cultural critics in particular treated East German artists with such kid gloves that anyone who produced anything but blatant government propaganda was hailed as a genius.

A West German Critic Looks Back in Bafflement

Suddenly, it dawned on us that the literature of the GDR, so successfully pushed for years, was by and large not worth a jot . . . *Ach*, I think today, *if only I'd just written a single little essay about why I wasn't interested in it.* But no, I can't claim that distinction. When GDR authors got prizes in the West, we all just smiled and said: Oh yes, the GDR bonus, of course.

Josef von Westphalen, *Von deutscher Bulimie*, 1990

In its last years, the GDR tried to claim that it was actually the real Germany: it made play with Martin Luther's memory, and suggested that the supposed Prussian virtues, if stripped of Junker militarism, were a positive alternative to the war-mongering *coca-colonialism* of the United States. This actually had a certain resonance with the hard German left. But then, anything anti-Western tends to have a certain resonance on the German hard left and right. Never more so than in the 1960s.

The Troubled Times

By 1960, West Germany was a pillar of NATO and the EEC. It had overtaken Britain as the world's second biggest car-maker and was positively inviting so-called *guest workers* (*Gastarbeiter*) from southern and eastern Europe to fill gaps in its labor force. Yet it was still a land of modest wages and modest consumption, where only half as many people actually owned cars as in Britain.

The times were a-changing, though, as a generation who had been grateful to work, save and forget the war was replaced by baby boomers who wanted it all—including the truth—right now.

Youth all over the west was impatient with boring, hypocritical, authoritarian elders. In Germany, the conflict was especially bitter because the older generation had sometimes been real Nazis. The *Frankfurt Auschwitz trials* of 1963–66 shocked young Germans. Vietnam outraged them. A strange constellation of revolt formed in some young heads: their wretched fathers were both ex-Nazis *and* slavish sidekicks of the capitalist west. One minute they'd been killing the Jews, the next they'd kowtowed to the *Amis*, leaving Germany a helpless consumer of *McKultur*. In the 1950s, *westernization* (*Westlichung*) had been widely seen as a positive thing, an alternative to Prussian or Nazi authoritarianism. Now, re-glossed as *westernification* (*Verwestlichung*), it started to carry

a negative connotation, opposition to which united hard left
and hard right.

> **The Place Extremes Meet**
>
> From late 1965 to the early 1970s, demonstrators carried
> placards with double-images of Lyndon B. Johnson and
> Adolf Hitler and equated the supposed *barbarism* of
> America's *cultural industry* with the barbarism of war . . .
> Any fancy idea seemed welcome provided it fitted into a
> rigid intellectual straightjacket of anti-Americanism . . .
> The slogan *USA-SA-SS* carried the day . . . In many cases,
> West German critics sounded like subscribers to an eastern
> propaganda machine.
>
> Bernd Greiner, *Saigon, Nuremberg, and the West:*
> *German Images of America in the Late 1960s*

This was the cultural sea in which swam the *Baader-Meinhof
gang/Red Army Fraction (RAF)* terror groups who, secretly
backed by the Stasi, appalled West Germany in the 1970s. It
helps, perhaps, to explain why one of their leading members,
Horst Mahler, later became a prominent neo-Nazi.

> Ulrike Meinhof and Gudrun Ensslin were young women
> students who had been deeply influenced by a morally
> rigid and radical Protestantism. The men, the magnetic
> and brutal Andreas Baader and the rootless Jan-Carl
> Raspe, were less intellectual and more impulsive. All came
> from middle-class backgrounds. Driven by hatred of the
> United States' "imperialist" war in Vietnam and of the
> "repressive" West German state, they never developed a
> coherent political ideology.
>
> *The New York Times,* January 3, 1988

The gang was born on June 2, 1967, when a West Berlin policeman (revealed many years later to have been in the pay of the Stasi) gunned down an unarmed demonstrator who was protesting against the visit of the Shah of Iran. Afterward, at a student meeting, Gudrun Ensslin declared: *This fascist state wants to kill us all! Violence is the only answer to violence. This is Generation Auschwitz, you can't argue with them!*

Germany was by no means the only place where the vague idealism of the 1960s rapidly curdled into violence. But Baader-Meinhof/RAF was unique in its hands-on personal viciousness, and uniquely troubling. At the height of its campaign, during the so-called *German Autumn* of 1977, when it was able to assassinate prominent figures like industry chief Hans-Martinn Schleyer and Dresdner Bank head Jürgen Ponto seemingly at will, and in a 1977 survey, one in four West Germans under 30 admitted to *a certain sympathy* with this group of messianic killers, who possessed no rationally definable goal other than freeing their own leaders from prison.

Why did so many people feel this sneaking sympathy? Certainly, anti-Americanism played a major part. But perhaps there was something older at work, too:

> Meinhof tried to explain the RAF's mission . . . They were not so blind as to think that they would bring about revolution in Germany, or that they would not be killed and imprisoned. The point was to "salvage historically the whole state of understanding attained by the movement of 1967–68; it was a case of not letting the struggle fall apart again". . . . These are words with long echoes in the German past . . . from the tradition of doomed struggle, fighting to the end in order to leave a message for the future.
>
> Neal Ascherson, *The Guardian*, September 28, 2008

Ascherson (who knew Meinhof personally) is surely right. In this worldview, whether we do any actual good to anyone in the here-and-now doesn't matter. What counts is simply the example we set, for some unknowable future, by sticking to our guns despite everything. It's a strange idea, when you think about it, and it's hard not to see it as somehow descended from Luther's notion that we're saved not by good works but *by faith alone* (*sola fide*).

Battleground Germany

Fortunately, throughout these years of nihilism, German politics was dominated not by a hero with his eye on the pathos of future justification, but by that classic center-left, chain-smoking, back-room deal-maker, Helmut Schmidt.

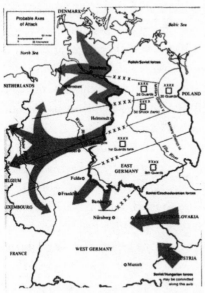

Under Schmidt, Germany dealt with its murderous terrorists without ever seriously undermining personal freedoms. He weathered the world economic crisis ushered in by the *1973 Oil Crisis*, by allowing borrowing to rise. German democracy emerged triumphant, while German industry and skillsets were saved.

The probable next big thing according to NATO, 1978.

Schmidt's run ended when he placed Germany too firmly in the Western camp for the taste of his own Social Democratic Party. This was at a time of massive East-West tension: in 1977, Schmidt warned NATO that a big Soviet upgrade of medium-range missiles was unbalancing things, making the nightmare scenario more likely. He suggested that the US should react in kind, while also negotiating.

Schmidt's party, though, had always been lukewarm about the Adenauer project of *binding to the West* (*Westbindung*). Some within it remained bafflingly convinced, despite the Russian invasions of Hungary (1956) and Czechoslovakia (1968), that the US was the more likely to start a shooting war. When the Americans agreed in 1979 to install some short-range land-based Pershing missiles in West Germany, large sections of the population exploded in protest. The modern Green Party was born out of this movement, which it's difficult to see as based merely on a rational fear of a US-initiated Armageddon. It seems more believable that Adenauer was right to worry about the lack of basic sympathy for *Westbindung* among some Germans. As one of the founders of the Green Party, Marieluise Beck, put it recently: *I did not, at the time, realise that the anti-Pershing campaign was only partly pacifist, and was also partly a deeply ambivalent protest movement against the USA and NATO.*

By 1982, Schmidt had lost so much support within his own party that he couldn't take it with him when he needed to tighten the budget. He went, and was replaced by the Christian Democrat Helmut Kohl, who was completely in agreement with Adenauer's line. Under Kohl, the US rockets appeared in Germany. The result was not Armageddon, but serious negotiations which in 1987 removed all American and Russian short-range missiles.

By then, everything had changed: Mikhail Gorbachev had taken over a post-1945 Russian Empire that was bankrupt and falling apart.

East Elbia Comes Back

At the start of 1989, Gorbachev or not, state bankruptcy or not, GDR boss Eric Honecker declared that the Wall would still be there *in fifty years, or a hundred years.* The regime confidently planned its 40th birthday party for October 7, 1989, and went on its nasty little way: China was openly praised for defending socialism in Tiananmen Square; German people were shot for trying to *desert the Republic*; and the Stasi was still training the last bastard offshoots of the Baader-Meinhof gang to carry out murders in the west.

In May, the Hungarian authorities started allowing people into Austria, and so on to Germany. Tens of thousands of East Germans scented the chance to escape, and booked holidays to Hungary. West German embassies in Budapest and Prague were suddenly crammed with asylum-claiming East Germans. On September 11, the Hungarians simply opened the gates. By the end of the month, 30,000 refugees had flooded into West Germany.

In desperation, the GDR closed the border to Czechoslovakia. At the state birthday party in East Berlin on October 6–7, 1989, Gorbachev, no fan of the East German hardliner, told Honecker that *life punishes anyone who arrives too late.*

The Goodbye Kiss

The crowds cheered *Gorbi*; after he'd left, the police beat them up. On October 9, in Leipzig, people gathered, determined but fearful: no one knew if the authorities would go for a *Peking Solution* (a massacre) or a *Polish Solution* (a compromise).

No one in the crowd threw bottles; no one in the police or army opened fire. On October 17, Honecker stood down and on November 3 the border with Czechoslovakia was reopened. In two days, 15,000 people fled East Germany. On November 9, apparently by accident, the Berlin Wall was declared open and was immediately overwhelmed by people going through it or taking hammers to it. Helmut Kohl himself had expected this so little that he was at a state banquet in Warsaw at the time.

Things were moving fast, but everyone assumed that for the time being East Germany would remain a separate state. After all, uniting would surely be an incredibly complex process, needing the involvement of all international partners and demanding full, open public debate within Germany, followed by an election specifically concerned with it.

There was nothing of the kind. A patriotic alliance led by the eastern branch of Kohl's CDU (a young Angela Merkel prominent within it) romped the new elections to the East German parliament in March 1990. Still no one had actually voted on unification, but the East Germans were voting with their feet. In January 1990 alone, 200,000 migrated to the West. The chant of the demonstrators in Leipzig was turning from patriotic appeal (*We are one people!*) to blackmail: *Bring us the Deutschmark, and we'll stay here—if not, we'll come and get it! (Kommt die D-Mark, bleiben wir, kommt sie nicht, geh'n wir zu ihr!)*

Fear of a new *Flight from the East* now drove things. If West Germany swapped the East-Mark for the Deutschmark at 1:1, it might keep people where they were. But how could any ex-East German state-run business pay such wages? How could the new regions afford near-parity of pensions and benefits? The consequence—huge subsidies needed from West Germany—was so predictable that Bundesbank president Otto Pöhl resigned over the issue. But Kohl's team was adamant. East Germany got the Deutschmark on July 1, 1990. West Germany was locked into paying to keep Germans in East Elbia (even though no peacetime government since 1850 had managed to stop them leaving).

Still there had been no vote on unification. It was domestic politics that made the final decision. The opinion polls all had Kohl on course for defeat at the next West German general election. But what if it wasn't just a *West* German election?

Extraordinarily, reunification took place on October 3, 1990, without either side, East or West, ever getting a vote on it. Many people argue that Kohl bought French agreement by promising—without telling his people—to soon give up the beloved Deutschmark and commit to the euro.

By permitting Germany to expand eastwards, Mitterand helped Kohl become the "Chancellor of Unity." This in turn put Kohl in a position to relieve Germany of its dearly held currency, one of the greatest triumphs of the Mitterand presidency.

Der Spiegel, September 30, 2010

Kohl played the patriotic bonus for all it was worth, promising another Economic Miracle that would turn the new states into *blooming landscapes*. Even so, in the general election of December 1990 he at best held on in West Germany, slipping compared to 1987 results in most areas. People were clearly underwhelmed by what the *Chancellor of Unity* had just done. In the East, of course, it was different: Kohl swept all the five new states, four by huge margins, and was easily able to lead a new coalition.

Now it came to the huge choice of whether parliament should shift from Bonn to Berlin. The long, tense debate on June 20, 1991 was too close to call, right to the end. When the division was called at last, MPs from the late West Germany voted for Bonn by 291 to 214. Many observers say that it was only an impassioned speech in favor of Berlin from Interior Minister Wolfgang Schäuble, wheelchair-bound after an attempt on his life only months earlier, which made it even that close.

As so often in German history, disunity was the West's downfall. The western MPs' vote for Bonn was clear—but not quite clear enough. Yet again, a near monocultural block of East Elbian votes, though far smaller in number, was able narrowly to swing the decision: the new states voted 80% for Berlin, so it fell out 320 to 328 in favor. The center of political gravity in Germany shifted from the old, once-Roman Rhineland to a city whose claim to be the national capital rested entirely on the idea that 1871 had been a genuine unification.

The shortest history of German politics since Fredrick the Great.

No Second Miracle

It soon seemed that West Germany might have bitten off—or rather, had stuffed into its mouth without being asked—more than it could chew. There'd never been a mysterious West German formula for *Wirtschaftwunder,* just the ruthless, free-market purgative dished out by Erhard under the uniquely handy circumstances of 1948. The currency union of 1990 was the opposite: good for short-term contentment, disastrous for business.

With wages, benefits, and pensions set at near-parity with the West, most East Germans decided to stay put. But since productivity was so much lower there, after decades of almost no investment, businesses could not compete. So western Germany had to foot the bill.

Just as they were from 1871 to 1933, the rich, productive western Germans were told that it was their national duty to subsidize the hopeless East Elbian economy and maintain a vast bureaucracy in their alleged capital, Berlin.

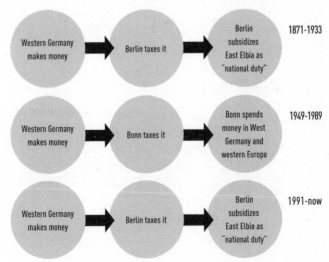

The shortest history of modern internal German tax flow.

Soon, they began to have doubts. Jokes started being told:

What's the difference between a Turk and an Ossi (East German)? The Turk speaks German and works.
Why are the Chinese so happy? They still have their Wall.

 The economy began to creak. In 1997, the all-new Mercedes A-Class flipped over during the elk test (*Elchtest*), designed to see if the car could make a sudden brake and turn; the word caught on and became proverbial because it seemed to show how Germany was losing the plot. By the end of the second millennium, bullish Blair-Bush trans-Atlanticists were certain that the future belonged to the Anglo-Saxon model:

As economic growth stalls yet again, Germany is being branded the sick man (or even the Japan) of Europe . . . Germany's weakness has, indeed, come at an especially awkward time for the euro. The new currency's almost uninterrupted slide against the dollar since its introduction in January owes much to gloom over the German economy . . . The level of subsidy to the east, which accounts for roughly 5% of overall German GDP, has barely fallen since 1990 . . . Germany is unlikely soon to shed its title as the sick man of Europe.

The Economist, June 3, 1999

The Third Millennium

While the freebooting Anglo-Saxons set off gleefully on a borrow-and-spend boom which turned out to be as solid as an Icelandic Bank, Germany quietly sorted itself out.

Another center-left deal-maker, Gerhard Schröder, brokered the systemic benefits shake-up of 2005, now proverbial in Germany as *Hartz IV*. These made it far less attractive to live long-term on state benefits, and pushed claimants toward the new *Jobcenters*, whose English title suggested where the idea came from. Schröder also persuaded his Green Party partners that if keeping Germany out of all wars meant allowing mass murder to happen in the Balkans, something had to give. He fixed the hard left by giving it hits of Americaphobia, crying that Germany would not join Gulf War II because it was *not available for adventures.* George W. Bush was furious; Schröder squeaked home for his second term.

By 2005, Germany wasn't looking sick at all. Southern Europeans spent overvalued euros on high-quality German goods, while their own, lower-priced alternatives gathered dust. The Far East was suddenly rich and its peoples wanted whatever rich Europeans wanted; their new industries also needed the custom-built machine tools, cranes, and conveyor-belts which German industry was matchless in producing. America gorged on imported German cars. In a world awash with credit, Germany worked flat out.

When people suddenly realized in 2008 that borrowed money is only borrowed, things could have been terrible for Germany. Instead, its recession lasted exactly a year. Germany betted big on the storm blowing over fast, and nursed its industrial base rather than letting it die. The fact that so much of German industry is (thanks largely to Erhardt in 1948) still owned by families rather than investment funds helped. Such people simply didn't want to stop being industrialists, even when things got tough. The state banks—who were often, as with VW, major shareholders in industry—stepped in to help. The unique West German tradition of genuine union-boss negotiation did the rest. Owners offered, and workers accepted, part-time work in lieu of unemployment.

It was a great call. When the rest of the world recovered, America was still addicted to imports; the Far East was still newly rich; even Europeans who now had to choose more carefully, carefully chose what they saw as quality products that would keep their value. At the height of the Greek debt crisis, people in Greece were burning German flags—but buying more German cars than ever as hedges in case they were forced out of the Euro.

Germany was looking incredibly stable and robust. For three elections in a row (2005, 2009, and 2013), Angela Merkel emerged as Chancellor; at each election she edged closer to that very rare thing in Germany, an overall majority of her own. The country was world *Exportmeister* and so trusted it could borrow money at zero interest. When people said that Europe needed to bail out its weaker states, they meant Germany; when America said Europe needed to stand up to Russia, it meant *Germany*; when British politicians demanded special concessions from *Europe*, they meant *Germany*.

German society worked, too. In terms of total personal wealth, surprisingly enough, the average German was worth less than the average Frenchman or Italian. This was largely because far fewer Germans owned their own homes, and many from the former East Germany had net worths of virtually zero. But as a distinguished economic historian pointed out, his countrymen weren't really poor at all, because they were part of a well-oiled body politic:

> The social state (*Sozialstaat*) is part of the wealth of the Germans . . . We live in a functioning commonwealth (*Gemeinwesen*) in which people don't need to rely as heavily on personal wealth as they do in other states in order to live securely and contentedly. Our wealth is not simply in the number of cars and houses we own.
>
> Werner Abelshauser, *Die Zeit*, March 27, 2013

Abelshauser's claim carried an implied warning. What if that quintessentially West German trust in the economy and public institutions weakened? Indeed, there were some signs that the rich were de-coupling from Abelshauser's *functioning commonwealth*. From 2012, Germans with money quite suddenly started to act more like Anglo-Saxons, piling into property and creating a house-price boom which outpaced even the notorious UK market. Private education—never remotely as important in Germany as in the UK or the US— suddenly took off. A new pro–free-market, anti-welfare, anti-Greek-bailout, EU-critical party was born: the *AfD* (*Alternative für Deutschland*). The founder, Bernd Lucke, was a university professor, as were half the people (many of them high-profile citizens) who publicly endorsed its first manifesto. The wealthy seemed to doubt the old certainties. What if the poor—*the 40% of Germans who in effect own nothing at all* (*Die Welt*)—were also to stop believing?

These, though, were mere noises off as Merkel triumphantly entered her third term. The only real trouble was, as ever, East Elbia.

The Insupportable East

Despite a colossal aid program, Kohl's promised *blooming landscapes* were still on life support. The cumulative figures were becoming quite astounding:

> In 1991 alone, 143 billion DM had to be transferred to eastern Germany to secure incomes, support businesses, and improve infrastructure . . . by 1999 the total amounted to 1.634 trillion Marks, and even taking back-flows into account, it was 1.2 trillion Marks net . . . The sums were so large that public debt in Germany more than doubled. This trend from the first years of German unification has not substantially altered to the present day.
>
> Federal Office of Political Education, June 23, 2009

This vast expenditure was having very little effect. True, Greater Berlin seemed to be booming. As the capital, it was a vast well of government spending; its grunge chic and cheap rents were beloved of tourists and start-ups. Yet it all rode on debt and subsidy. Berlin (pop. 4m) had far greater state debts than Bavaria (pop. 12.5m) despite receiving roughly 3.5bn euro annually from central government. Every other European capital city helped to fund its country; only in Germany was it the other way around.

Deep in East Elbia proper, things were catastrophic. The population of Bavaria rose by 8% between 1991 and 2012; in Saxony-Anhalt it fell by 20%. In the dry language of the Federal Ministry of the Economy and Energy in a 2016 report: *this demographic situation is unique in Europe and internationally*. Even two trillion Euros could not, it turns out, buck the fact that East Elbia was still, as it had been since 1850, a place where, given the choice, most Germans just didn't want to live.

The drain was officially predicted to continue, and since the people leaving East Elbia were disproportionately young, educated and female, the reality on the ground was set to be even worse than the bare numbers sounded.

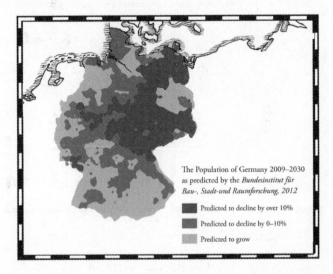

The Population of Germany 2009–2030 as predicted by the *Bundesinstitut für Bau-, Stadt-und Raumforschung, 2012*

Predicted to decline by over 10%

Predicted to decline by 0–10%

Predicted to grow

Once again, try drawing those two lines—the *limes* of 100 AD and the Elbe—across this map of the probable German future.

Those who remained—progressively older, less educated and more male—voted quite differently from the west. When Germany's main national poll of voting intentions (Infratest's *Sunday Question—die Sonntagsfrage*) came out, the data was always broken down into two geographical areas, *Westdeutschland* and *Ostdeutschland*. It had to be, or the results would have been misleading. In 2005 and 2009, East Elbian voters put the NPD (*Nationaldemokratische Partei Deutschlands*), a party which is all but openly neo-Nazi, into two state parliaments. And while significant numbers voted for the extreme right, far larger numbers voted for *Die Linke*, the closest descendant of the old GDR-ruling Communist party. Again, the geographical divide is central, so maps are the best witness:

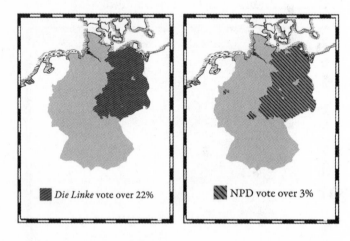

Strongholds of the hard left and neo-Nazi right, 2013.

It would be easy to ascribe this only to the Soviet occupation from 1949 to 1989. But East Elbia has been voting differently for generations. It voted disproportionately for the old *Konservative Partei* before wwi, for the DNVP in Weimar, for the Nazis in 1930–33, and, by 2009, for extremists of both left and right.

Nostalgia for the old East Germany—*Ostalgie*, as it was known—might be a harmless, ironic tourist experience for most Germans, but there seemed to be more than a few people in Saxony or Pomerania who had a more troubling and serious longing for a kind of German-ness that had nothing to do with western values or alliances.

Still, in 2015 safe, secure, prosperous Germany seemed able to live with being shackled once again to an economically moribund and politically unnerving East Elbia. Merkel's domestic approval rating in April of that year was 75%—astonishing, for a democratic leader ten years in power. She'd been tough on Greece, and was disliked in much of southern Europe, but the new East European EU states and her own voters only applauded her for it.

Then, in September 2015, she drove the *functioning commonwealth* of German society—and the whole EU—straight into her very own elk-test.

Merkel's Strange Autumn

The Dublin Treaty of 1997 says that asylum seekers to the EU must register, and therefore remain, in the first country they enter. In September 2015, as refugees streamed north and west out of the conflict zones of Iraq and Syria, Angela Merkel unilaterally voided it. This turned Germany into the number one goal for the dispossessed of the Middle East.

It's not clear why she did it. Maybe out of a sense of moral obligation: a genuine desire to help the refugees and to ease the pressure on Greece and Italy. Perhaps she saw the incomers as much-needed young blood for Germany's aging population. Or it might have been a more complex political feint. Her own party had long been trying to refuse asylum-seekers from Albania, Montenegro, and Kosovo—on the grounds that these were now *safe states of origin*—and had always been blocked by their SPD partners in the coalition. Some think Merkel calculated that by taking the lead on refugees from the civil war in Syria, she could steal the moral high ground on this issue.

Whatever her motivation, the effect was to unilaterally declare southeastern Europe a transit camp for asylum seekers wanting to reach Germany, a country whose smiling leader famously offered them selfies. It seems clear that Merkel seriously miscalculated how large the numbers would become, or how much resistance she would face from other EU countries.

The *welcome culture* (*Willkommenskultur*) of many Germans amazed the world, but it soon reached its limits in the face of mounting evidence that only a minority of the huge influx were were actually families who'd fled immediate peril in Syria—or even Syrians at all. On New Year's Eve 2015, widely reported scenes of mass sexual harassment in Cologne by young men of *Arab or North African origin* (as the police put it) seemingly without fear of the German authorities, sounded the death knell for the open door policy.

Merkel continued to intone the mantra *We can cope* (*Wir schaffen das*) while demanding that other EU countries take some of the refugees in. No one except Sweden responded, and even Sweden soon closed its doors again. In Eastern Europe, the reaction was especially bitter.

When Angela Merkel opened Germany's borders to the refugees trapped in Budapest last September, she was at the zenith of her power. But in Europe, her austerity demands had turned many countries against her—and here she was imposing her refugee principles, a curious mixture of Protestant parsonage and German sensibility, on the Continent. The price for her policies is not just the rise of a new right-wing populist party in Germany and a German society that is more divided and disgruntled than it has been in years. She has also created a Europe that is no longer united.

Der Spiegel, March 10, 2016

That new *right-wing populist party* was the *AfD*, which during 2015 mutated into something uncomfortably close to the neo-Nazi NPD. In 2016, it took 15.1% in prosperous, southwestern Baden-Württemberg. On the face of things, it seemed that nowhere was safe. But "B-W" famously has its own religious divide (the Allies created it in 1949 out of three different realms) and if you look at that 2016 election on a map, it's as it was in all Germany from 1930–33: the radical right clearly does best in protestant areas. As with Hitler— as with Brexit and Trump—what makes people vulnerable to wild scares and promises isn't just income, but culture. East Elbia, with its centuries-old mix of colonial fears and Lutheran authoritarianism, is well-dunged land: there, the *AfD* won 24% (Saxony-Anhalt) and 20.9% (Mecklenburg-Vorpommern). In both, the *NPD* took 3%, too. No subsidy, not even two trillion Euros since 1990—a Greek bailout every year—can buy off an ancient mindset.

After an attack on a home for asylum seekers, one headline in *Die Welt* suggested in February 2016 that it wasn't immigrants who had a problem with assimilating into German culture, but Saxons (Saxons is widely used in western Germany to mean all eastern Germans). When the October 3 *Day of Unity* celebrations in Dresden were ruined by neo-Nazi firebombs in the run-up and hard-right demonstrations on the day itself, Germany's broadsheets, liberal and conservative, wondered out loud whether the Saxons were really a different people. What on earth was going on in east German heads? A despairing joke said it all: if Europe can have a Brexit, why can't Germany have a *Säxit*?

In December 2016, there was no joking, only despair at the deadly truck attack on a Berlin Christmas market, carried out by a failed asylum seeker who, in the view of most Germans, should long since have been deported. Powered by anger, the *AfD* broke out of its East Elbian strongholds in the 2017 elections. People in the former East German states voted even more heavily for the *Alternative für Deutschland* than expected. In Saxony it became the strongest party, scoring 27%. If this had been repeated across the whole of Germany, it would be truly worrying. But of course it wasn't. As ever, the East had voted differently. Nationally, the *AfD* vote was only 12.6%—a shock, certainly, but only a danger if the established parties who represent 74% of Germans now lose their nerve.

Conclusion: 2019 and the Real History of Germany

There's no point studying the past unless it sheds some light on the present. As the West grapples with crisis after crisis, the story of Germany carries a clear message. The brief Prussian/Nazi era of German history—1866–1945—must finally be seen for what it was: a terrible aberration.

Since 100 AD, southwestern Germany has belonged to Western Europe. It was only in 1525 that a new, essentially non-western Germany appeared on the scene: Prussia. The western Germans, meanwhile, were so far from being natural warmongers—or inherent state-worshippers—that they were unable to unite. More and more, their lands became battlefields and potential colonies for their stronger neighbors. Then, in 1814, Prussia, at that time a mere client of Russia, was massively strengthened by an epochal stroke of folly. Britain, which, like Trumpists today, positively wanted Europe to remain a mess of competing states, gifted it a modern industrial region on the Rhine. In 1866, southwestern Germany was defeated in battle, and shortly afterward absorbed, by this fatally muscled-up Prussia, a country which, by most of the normal standards of European nationhood—history, geography, political arrangements, religion—was entirely foreign. This was the great deformation. Henceforth, all the wealth, industry and man-power of southern and western Germany were channeled into Prussian ambition. This aimed always at one thing above all: hegemony over Poland, the Baltic lands, and northern central Europe, in alliance with Russia if possible, through a show-down with Russia if need be. The millennial struggle ended in 1945 with the blood-soaked extinction of Prussia, down to its very name. Western Germany was free at last. In 1949, it finally became a true political entity.

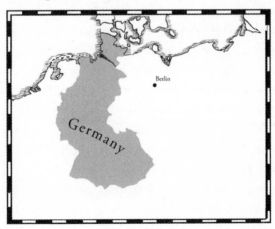

West Germany (1949–90) was extraordinarily similar to Germania as planned by Caesar Augustus c. 1 AD, to East Francia at the Treaty of Verdun in 843 AD, and to the Confederation of the Rhine in 1808.

The Germany of Konrad Adenauer, Willy Brandt, and Helmut Schmidt wasn't some half-baked provisional country, waiting mournfully for its other half. Unlike that passing monster, Prussia-Germany, it had genuine roots.

A single political unit with its eastern border on the Elbe and its capital on the Rhine, where *Germany's windows are wide open to the West . . . among the vineyards* (Adenauer) was the culmination of Germany's true history: a place clearly distinct from the Mediterranean lands, yet beyond all doubt an integral part of the West.

In 1991, though, the vineyards were abandoned for Berlin, which is nearer to Warsaw than it is to Mainz or Stuttgart. It turned out that there was a Prussian specter haunting Germany after all: the victors of 1866 were still quietly ghostwriting its history. The so-called *reunification* merely recreated a lopped-off version of the so-called German Empire, that Prussian lie which was foisted on western Germans, and the world, by Bismarck in 1871. Too many people didn't think twice: they instinctively supported this alleged reunification; they assumed, without asking why, that Berlin was their natural capital; they agreed that it was their national duty to subsidize a bankrupt East Elbia, just as their ancestors had been forced to do under the Junkers and the Nazis. Few Germans in 1990 realized that they were singing along to a half-remembered Prussian tune.

Recalling this story might now help Germans to look, as Adenauer did, to their true friends, and indeed their true interests, before it's too late. Germany—western Germany, in practice—runs a colossal trade surplus, not least with the Eurozone itself. In 2018, it maintained the world's largest accounts surplus for the third year in a row at $299 billion.

As a result, the German government can get credit at astonishingly low rates. The 2016 issue of ten-year German bonds offered *negative* interest, and still sold, meaning that international investors pay Germany to hold their money. Yet instead of offering itself as guarantor for some kind of a common Eurobond, Germany insists on financial rectitude from its vital neighbors, its export markets, and its natural friends, while itself pouring trillions—*trillions*—of Euros into the East Elbia that was so often its nemesis. This is Prussia, speaking from beyond the grave.

Unlike the peoples who actually border Russia, East Elbians on both political extremes have a notable tendency to think of Moscow as a more natural partner, a closer spiritual brother, than Washington or Paris. This, if it needs saying again, is an idea that has nothing to do with German history and everything to do with Prussian history. The rump East Elbia no longer has enough votes to swing all-German politics as it did in 1930–33, but those millions of anti-Western voices are a serious new weight in the scale.

Germany's former Foreign Minister, Joschka Fischer, is no unthinking disciple of Adenauer (he made his name in the 1960s by leading hard-left demonstrations), but he now invokes that memory:

> The *AfD* represents German right-wing nationalists (and worse) who want to return to the old man-in-the-middle position and forge a closer relationship with Russia. Cooperation between the *CDU* and *AfD* would betray Adenauer's legacy and be tantamount to the end of the Bonn Republic . . . Meanwhile, there is similar danger from the other side . . . *Die Linke* (the Left Party), some

of whose leading members effectively want the same thing as the *AfD*: closer relations with Russia and looser or no integration with the West. One hopes that we will be spared this tragic future, and that Merkel will retain her office beyond 2017. The future of Germany, Europe, and the West may depend on it.

Angela Merkel did win again. She and Emmanuel Macron had a chance to revive the EU's Franco-German core. But it hasn't happened. It must, though it won't be easy. The relative strengths of France and Germany are very different now from in the days of de Gaulle and Adenauer. "Reunification" has massively redirected Germany's attention to East Elbia. Bonn was physically close to Paris, Brussels, The Hague, even London; Berlin is closer to Prague and Warsaw. Trump's wavering on NATO, Britain's exit from the EU, and hostility to Germany from southern Europe can only encourage the idea that staying *bound to the West* is no longer central to Germany's future.

Merkel's successor must hold firm and recall the Roman *limes*; Charlemagne's renaissance; the golden age of medieval Germany; the southwestern realms that fought in vain against Prussia in 1866; the hapless southern and western Germans shackled by Bismarck to war against Russia; the doomed southern and western Germans who never voted for Hitler but got him just the same; and Adenauer's late, lamented West Germany. The West must reciprocate by seeing that 1871–1945 was a Prussian anomaly in the story of the country between the Rhineland, the Elbe and the Alps, where state worship, puritanical zeal and scar-faced militarism have always been entirely alien.

This Germany is the sole hope for Europe. It must now act, and it must now be embraced, as what it was always meant to be: a mighty land at the very heart of the West.

Postscript, March 2019

After the elections of September 2017, all this only became more urgent. Once again: The *AfD* scored 12.6% nationally—by a bizarre coincidence, the same as UKIP (the UK Independence Party) in Britain in 2015—but this soared to 27% in Saxony, making it the largest party there.

What if this spreads? History can reassure Germany. Don't panic, as David Cameron did when he looked at that UKIP 12.6%. Western and eastern Germany have always been different places. We need to start looking at German politics the way we look at America. It's about cultural history, and Germany's fault line along the Elbe is far older and deeper than the Civil War divide in the US. Saxony isn't going to become like the Rhineland any more than Mississippi is going to go Democrat. That sounds drastic, but there's a huge upside: Saxony's politics won't spread to southwest Germany any more than California will swing Republican.

The 2018 results from Bavaria (10.2%) and Hesse (13%) back this up. In the east, the *AfD* continues to rise—the latest detailed Infratest poll (September 6, 2018) puts it on 27% in the region as whole. Add to that the 18% that Die Linke scores, and 45% of all voters in the former East Germany intend to vote for anti-EU, anti-NATO parties. But in the West, those figures are only 14% and 8% respectively. There is a cultural watershed that the *AfD* simply cannot cross. And because the east is now so much smaller than in the

Weimar Republic (and its population falling), what happens there just doesn't have the clout, any more, to swing national politics—so long as that national politics holds it nerve.

Seventy-four percent of all Germans still intend to vote for pro-EU, pro-NATO parties. So, as Germany faces life without Angela Merkel, the lesson of history is clear. Western Germany should stop wasting money trying to please a region that will never be pleased. Like in the US, the great western parties should see that political homogeneity is not a prerequisite of a functioning democracy. Because the German system counts up all the vote nationally, not by states, they should concentrate on winning big in the places where they can win big. If that leaves the east struggling with a big *AfD* presence, well, so be it. Better that than deform the whole of German politics by trying to please middle-aged single men in Saxony who (like the Trump core) are never going to be pleased by anything centrist liberals do.

Western Germany—the heart of Europe—must now concentrate on taking care of itself, and finding a vision that will unite it. Crisis? Not if the Germans understand their own history. And it is time, now more than ever, for us all to understand the real history of Germany.

ACKNOWLEDGMENTS

They often say real editors no longer exist in British publishing. Ben Yarde-Buller is the living disproof, and I bless the day that my agent, Caspian Dennis, took his call. It was a great pleasure to work with James Nunn on the graphics, and with Matt Baylis, whose suggestions were always useful and sometimes lifesaving. Vital talks and correspondence were had with Dr Peter Thompson, Professor Karen Leeder (Oxford University), Professor Stefan Szymanksi (University of Michigan) and Dr Matthew Fitzpatrick (Flinders University). Peter Thompson also took many of the photographs—I am very grateful to Oxford Brookes University for helping to fund my trip with him. The picture of the Bismarck memorial in Hamburg was specially taken by Philip v. Oppen. My mother, Janet Hawes née Fry, rightly insisted on an important rewrite. I have had many fascinating conversations about German history with my father-in-law, Karl v. Oppen, and with his daughter, my beloved wife, Dr Karoline v. Oppen (University of Bath), who has lived with this book for far too long.

PERMISSIONS ACKNOWLEDGMENTS

Every effort has been made to identify and contact copyright holders. Please note that despite best efforts some rights holders of a few images could not be determined. If an error or omission is brought to our notice, we will be pleased to correct the situation in future editions of this book. For further information, please contact the publisher.

p. 10: Eduard Bendemann / Wikimedia Commons / Public Domain / Grayscaled from original

p. 13: Carole Raddato / CC BY-SA 2.0 / Grayscaled from original

p. 14: Allison Sermarini's Maps of the Ancient World / Encyclopaedia Biblica

p. 15: Gustav Droysen / Wikimedia Commons / Public Domain / Grayscaled from original

p. 21: © Nino Barbieri / Wikimedia Commons / CC BY-SA 3.0 / GFDL / Grayscaled from original

p. 22: Felix Dahn / Spiegel Online

p. 25: (top) Carole Raddato / CC-BY-SA-2.0 / Grayscaled from original; (bottom left) © Classical Numismatic Group / CC BY 3.0 / Grayscaled from original; (bottom right) Coin depicting Flavius Theodoricus (Theodoric the Great) / CC BY 3.0 / Grayscaled from original

p. 33: © PHGCOM / Wikimedia Commons / CC BY-SA 3.0 / GFDL / Grayscaled from original

p. 47: Life of the Countess Matilda of Canossa / Public Domain

p. 52: Public Domain

p. 53: (top) © Friedrichsen / Wikimedia Commons / CC BY-SA 3.0 / Grayscaled from original; (bottom) Meister Des Codex Manesse / Public Domain

p. 64: Portrait of Martin Luther by Lucas Cranach the Elder / Public Domain

p. 67: Anton Woensam / Public Domain

p. 72: Equestrian Portrait of Charles V by Titian / Public Domain

p. 76: Scene from the Grandes Misères de la Guerre by Jacques Callot / Public Domain

p. 80: © Suse / Wikimedia Commons / CC BY-SA 3.0 / GFDL / Grayscaled from original

p. 133: Imagno / Getty Images

p. 134: © Janet Hartl / Wikimedia Commons / Public Domain

p. 138: (top) German Military "Oberbefehlshabers Ost" / Wikimedia Commons / Public Domain; (bottom) © Florian Horsthemke / Wikimedia Commons / CC BY 3.0 / Grayscaled from original

p. 139: Ginschel / FM Hindenburg and Ludendorff / Public Domain

p. 141: Public Domain

p. 144: © Bundesarchiv Bild 183-J0908-0600-002 / CC-BY-SA 3.0 / Grayscaled from original

p. 149: © Bundesarchiv Bild 102-00910 / CC-BY-SA 3.0 / Grayscaled from original

p. 155: Reichsbankdirektorium Berlin / National Numismatic Collection, National Museum of American History / Public Domain

p. 156: ullstein bild Dtl. / Getty Images

p. 158: (top) "Bauhaus Dessau 2005 main building from the south" / Wikimedia Commons / CC BY-SA 3.0 / GFDL / Public Domain; (bottom) © Jörg Zägel / Wikimedia Commons / CC BY-SA 3.0 / Grayscaled from original

p. 160: (top) Eddie Gerald / Alamy Stock Photo; (middle) © F. W. Murnau / Wikimedia Commons / Public Domain; (bottom) Public Domain

p. 163: FALKENSTEINFOTO / Alamy Stock Photo

p. 167: (left) Shawshots / Alamy Stock Photo; (right) Süddeutsche Zeitung Photo / Alamy Stock Photo

p. 170: Universal History Archive / Getty Images

p. 173: Klaus Niermann / Wikimedia Commons / Public Domain

p. 180: © A. Savin / Wikimedia Commons / CC BY-SA 3.0 / Grayscaled from original

p. 182: © NoTABENE / Wikimedia Commons / CC BY-SA 4.0 / Grayscaled from original

p. 187: Roger-Viollet / Getty Images

p. 207: dpa Picture-Alliance / Alamy Stock Photo

INDEX

ABOUT THE AUTHOR

James Hawes studied German at University of Oxford and University College London, then held lectureships in German at the universities of Maynooth, Sheffield, and Swansea. He has published six novels with Jonathan Cape. *Speak for England* (2005) predicted Brexit; it has been adapted for the screen by Andrew Davies, though not yet filmed. His last book, *Englanders and Huns*, was shortlisted for the Political Books of the Year Awards in 2015. He leads the MA in creative writing at Oxford Brookes University.